A Year of
Seasonal
dishes

FOOD&HOME
ENTERTAINING

First published in 2016 by Human & Rousseau,
an imprint of NB Publishers,
a division of Media24 Boeke (Pty) Ltd,
40 Heerengracht, Cape Town 8001

Commissioning editor: Annake Müller
Editor: Sean Fraser
Proofreader: Glynne Newlands
Cover image and other pictures: *Food & Home Entertaining*
Contributing photographers: Francois Booyens, Graeme Borchers, Sean Calitz, Neil Corder, Myburgh du Plessis,
Adel Ferreira, Clinton Friedman, Curtis Gallon, Vanessa Grobler, Christoph Heierli, Micky Hoyle, Michael le Grange,
Vanessa Lewis, Neville Lockhart, Lee Malan, Toby Murphy, Annalize Nel, Shane Powell, Roelene Prinsloo, Karl Rogers,
Craig Scott, Russell Smith, Dylan Swart, Bruce Tuck, Andrea van der Spuy, Dawie Verwey, Riana Vogel, Henrique Wilding,
Katelyn Williams, Graeme Wyllie, Elsa Young
Additional pictures: Pages 320 – 331: Claire Gunn; picture of Andrea (Welcome): Dylan Swart
Food contributors: Marwan al Sayed, Nicola Basson, Abbi Ben Yehudin, Ian Bergh, Shelly Bergh, Alex Bishop, Ingrid Casson,
Kelly Chrystal, Lisa Clark, Vicki Clarke, Vicky Crease, Sarah Dall, Vickie de Beer, Yavanna Dettremerie, Elizabeth Downes,
Helena Erasmus, Jacques Erasmus, Claire Ferrandi, Tracy Foulkes, Nikki Gaskell, Nicky Gibbs, Dirk Gieselmann, Sue Greig,
Kim Hoepfl, Thomas Hughes, Kanyacilla Hunt, Taryne Jakobi, Clive Johnson, Kevin Joseph, Gizelle Kennel, Colette le Clus,
Rudi Liebenberg, Tina Maritz, Thulisa Martins, Jules Mercer, Leigh Miles, Tomi Miller, Nomvuselelo Mncube, Anna Montali,
Cheyne Morrisby, Alfred Nxayi, Stefan Predorf, Rozanne Preston, Reuben Riffel, Neil Roake, Peter Rose, Anke Roux,
Angela Ridge, Leila Saffarian, Toni Scorgie, Lerato Shilakoe, Karen Short, Tara Sloggett, Quentin Spickernell, Michelle Theron,
Louise Thomas, Robyn Timson, Liam Tomlin, Hope Tshabangu, Illanique van Aswegen, Leandri van der Wat, Seline van der Wat,
Nadine Waner, Nikki Wefelmeier, Katelyn Williams, Odette Williams, Lyn Woodward, Katelynne Wooldridge, Gordon Wright
Contributing dietician: Maryke Gallagher
Book and cover design: The Suits Communications

Reproduction by Resolution Colour (Pty) Ltd, Cape Town
Printed and bound by CTP Printers, Cape Town

ISBN: 978-0-7981-7189-2

Contents

April

May

June

July

August

September

October

November

December

WELCOME

I f you're not already a reader of *Food & Home Entertaining* magazine, South Africa's most established culinary title, the good news is there's a lot more where this comes from in the form of our monthly publication filled with irresistible recipes for everyone from aspiring home cooks to accomplished chefs.

On the other hand, if you are a regular or occasional reader of the magazine, we hope the delicious dishes in *Food & Home Entertaining: A Year of Seasonal Dishes* – a compilation of the best of 10 years of *Food & Home Entertaining* – fill you with nostalgia and cravings you simply have to satisfy!

While I may be the *Food & Home Entertaining* editor who is lucky enough to write this letter, this cookbook would not have been possible without the legacy of the magazine's previous custodians, who have poured their creative energy and inspired direction into it – from first editor, the entrepreneurial Christine Cashmore to chef extraordinaire Angela Richardson, to the visionary Leigh Herringer, the super-stylish Jacquie Myburgh-Chemaly

and the pragmatic Rosanne Buchanan, these dynamic women all nurtured and raised *Food & Home Entertaining* to be the respected title it is today. Therefore, it is on their shoulders I stand.

Of course, a big thank you also goes to the food editors, stylists and photographers who have all brought the pages of *Food & Home Entertaining* to fruition and, in turn, *Food & Home Entertaining: A Year of Seasonal Dishes*.

When deciding on the flow and format of this beautiful cookbook, it seemed only fitting to remain true to the frequency and style of *Food & Home Entertaining* magazine. Hence, in the following pages, you will find a chapter for every month of the year, each one filled with 12 dishes that serve up a variety of flavours and cuisines to appeal to every palate and occasion – that's a total of 144 recipes! What's more – in keeping with *Food & Home Entertaining's* core philosophy of making your life easier – we have also included a handy seasonality chart (page 320) and a labour-of-love quantity conversion chart (page 326) to assist any measuring and weighing dilemmas you might have.

So, without further ado, prepare to dive into the tantalising 'smorgasbord' of *Food & Home Entertaining: A Year of Seasonal Dishes*. May it inspire, delight and leave you wanting more. Enjoy!

Andrea

Andrea Pafitis-Hill
Editor
Food & Home Entertaining
www.foodandhome.co.za

 FOODANDHOMEENTERTAININGMAGAZINESA   FHEMAG

 FOODANDHOMEMAG   FOODANDHOMESA

THE MONTH OF *January*

WHAT BETTER THAN TO KICK-START THE NEW YEAR ON A HEALTHY
NOTE! TAKE A LOOK AT OUR SELECTION OF LIGHTER DISHES,
BRIMMING WITH FLAVOUR AND PERFECT FOR WINDING DOWN
AFTER THE SEASON OF INDULGENCE. GET THAT BRAAI GOING,
INVITE FRIENDS AND FAMILY ROUND, AND SET UP YOUR
FLAVOURFUL FEAST IN THE GARDEN. HAPPY NEW YEAR!

Mint-and-lime tequila cooler

RECIPE AND STYLING BY **INGRID CASSON** PHOTOGRAPH BY **BRUCE TUCK**

Serves 10 EASY 1 hr 30 mins

THE FLAVOUR COMBINATIONS
**1 medium bunch of mint leaves +
extra, to garnish
105g (½ cup) castor sugar
125ml (½ cup) fresh lime juice
375ml (1½ cups) tequila
ice cubes, to serve
soda water, to serve
lime slices, to garnish**

HOW TO DO IT
1 Muddle the mint leaves with the castor sugar and fresh lime juice in a large shaker. Strain into a small jug and stir in the tequila.

2 Fill six tall glasses with ice and pour the cocktail over the ice cubes. Top with soda water, garnish with mint leaves and lime slices, and serve.

11

Parma ham, blueberry and feta salad

RECIPE AND STYLING BY **VICKI CLARKE** AND **NIKKI GASKELL** PHOTOGRAPH BY **ELSA YOUNG**

Serves 2 **EASY** 5 mins

THE FLAVOUR COMBINATIONS
1 packet baby salad leaves
70g Danish feta, crumbled
3 spring onions, thinly
sliced lengthways
150g fresh blueberries
10 thin slices Parma ham
white balsamic vinegar, to serve
olive oil, to serve

HOW TO DO IT
1 Combine the salad leaves, feta, spring onions and blueberries in a bowl, and top with the ham.
2 Serve drizzled with the vinegar and oil.

gluten + wheat FREE

The lovely Middle-Eastern flavour of the hummus dressing is great with the 'meaty' aubergines and sweet, tender tomatoes.

Baby aubergines, roasted tomato and avocado salad with hummus dressing

RECIPE AND STYLING BY **ILLANIQUE VAN ASWEGEN** PHOTOGRAPH BY **ADEL FERREIRA** ASSISTED BY **JASMARI FERREIRA**

Serves 4 EASY 1 hr

THE FLAVOUR COMBINATIONS
4 whole tomatoes
olive oil, to drizzle
salt and freshly ground black pepper, to taste
6 – 8 baby aubergines, halved
60ml (¼ cup) olive oil
2 pitas
2 avocados, sliced, to serve
60g baby salad leaves, to serve

DRESSING
180g tinned chickpeas, drained
2,5ml (½ tsp) garlic, crushed
15ml (1 tbsp) sesame seeds, toasted
5ml (1 tsp) sweet chilli sauce
15ml (1 tbsp) lemon juice
2,5ml (½ tsp) smooth peanut butter
45ml (3 tbsp) olive oil
30ml (2 tbsp) hot water
2,5ml (½ tsp) ground cinnamon
pinch of paprika

HOW TO DO IT

1 Preheat the oven to 190°C. Place the whole tomatoes on a roasting tray, drizzle with olive oil and season. Roast until tender, 20 – 25 minutes.

2 Toss the baby aubergines and the 60ml (¼ cup) olive oil together, coating as much of the flesh as possible with oil.

3 Heat a griddle pan until hot. Fry the aubergines until lightly charred, about 1 minute per side. Keep an eye on them so they don't burn.

4 Transfer the aubergines to a roasting tray and season. Roast in the oven until tender, 10 – 12 minutes.

5 For the pita croutons, turn the oven down to 180°C. Break the pitas into bite-size pieces, drizzle with olive oil and bake in the oven until golden and crisp, 10 – 12 minutes.

6 For the dressing, place all of the ingredients in a food processor and blend until smooth. Season and dilute with more water if necessary, until you have a pouring consistency.

7 Arrange the aubergines and tomatoes on four individual plates. Add a few avocado slices and baby salad leaves. Scatter the pita croutons on top. Serve with the dressing on the side.

15

Editor's choice

Snoek and summer peaches with herb remoulade

RECIPE AND STYLING BY **JACQUES ERASMUS** PHOTOGRAPH BY **MYBURGH DU PLESSIS**

Serves 4 **EASY** 30 mins

THE FLAVOUR COMBINATIONS
REMOULADE
1 egg
12,5ml Dijon mustard
2,5ml (½ tsp) garlic, finely chopped
200ml canola oil
30ml (2 tbsp) white wine vinegar
30g spring onions, chopped
25ml fresh flat-leaf parsley, chopped
45ml dill gherkin, chopped
1 hard-boiled egg, chopped
70g double-thick Greek yoghurt
Tabasco, to taste
salt and freshly ground black
pepper, to taste

2 medium snoek, butterflied
6 dessert peaches, halved
melted butter, for brushing
50ml maple syrup

HOW TO DO IT

1 Light a charcoal fire and allow to burn to coals.

2 For the remoulade, place the egg, mustard and garlic in a bowl and add the oil in three batches, whisking continuously. Stir in the vinegar. You should have a thick mayonnaise.

3 Stir in the spring onions, parsley, dill gherkin, hard-boiled egg and yoghurt. Season generously with Tabasco, salt and pepper.

4 Brush the fish and peaches with melted butter.

5 Grill the fish over the hot coals, about 12 minutes on each side, depending on the thickness of the fish. Grill the peaches until just soft, 7 – 8 minutes on each side.

6 Glaze the peaches with the maple syrup and allow to cook for a further 2 – 3 minutes over the coals to caramelise and char slightly.

7 Top the grilled fish with the peaches and serve with the herb remoulade.

Moroccan beef fillet with pomegranate-and-chilli couscous

RECIPE AND STYLING BY **TARYNE JAKOBI** PHOTOGRAPH BY **VANESSA LEWIS**

Serves 6 EASY 1 hr

THE FLAVOUR COMBINATIONS
1kg beef fillet

RUB
100g brown sugar
50g sea salt
5ml (1 tsp) ground cumin
5ml (1 tsp) ground coriander
5ml (1 tsp) mustard seeds
5ml (1 tsp) garlic salt

COUSCOUS
250ml (1 cup) chicken stock, hot
200g couscous
rubies of 1 pomegranate
1 red chilli, seeded and
finely chopped

DRESSING
30ml (2 tbsp) pomegranate
concentrate
5ml (1 tsp) wholegrain mustard
15ml (1 tbsp) verjuice
30ml (2 tbsp) olive oil

HOW TO DO IT

1 Mix together all of the ingredients for the rub and coat the fillet well. Leave to rest for 20 minutes at room temperature.

2 Heat the oven grill to high and cook the fillet, turning frequently, for about 20 minutes for medium-rare. Remove from oven and rest for 10 minutes.

3 Pour the stock over the couscous, cover and leave to stand until all of the water is absorbed. Break up the couscous with a fork and toss through the pomegranate rubies and chilli.

4 Whisk together all of the dressing ingredients until well combined.

5 Serve the fillet on the couscous, drizzled with the dressing.

dairy FREE

Lamb-and-nectarine kebabs

RECIPE AND STYLING BY **TONI SCORGIE** AND **NADINE WANER** PHOTOGRAPH BY **GRAEME WYLLIE**

Makes 16 **EASY** 50 mins +
extra, to soak and marinate

THE FLAVOUR COMBINATIONS
HARISSA PASTE
(makes about 350ml)

80g dried red chillies, chopped
250ml (1 cup) water, for soaking
10ml (2 tsp) cumin seeds
2,5ml (½ tsp) coriander seeds
5ml (1 tsp) cardamom pods
2,5ml (½ tsp) caraway seeds
3 garlic cloves, crushed
50ml tomato paste
100ml olive oil

KEBABS

90ml harissa paste (see above)
640g lamb leg, cubed
4 large ripe nectarines, quartered
100g fresh mint leaves
15ml (1 tbsp) olive oil, for brushing

HOW TO DO IT

1 For the harissa paste, place the chillies in a bowl, cover with the water and leave to soak for at least 2 hours. Drain, reserving the water for later use, and set aside.

2 Heat a non-stick pan over low heat and dry-fry the cumin, coriander and cardamom until fragrant. Remove from heat and allow to cool, then grind in a pestle and mortar, together with the caraway seeds.

3 Place the garlic, drained chillies and about 100ml of the reserved soaking water in a food processor and blend to a smooth paste. Add the crushed spices and tomato paste and blend until well combined.

4 Slowly pour in the 100ml olive oil, blending continuously until all of the oil is incorporated and the paste is smooth. The excess will keep for about a month in an airtight sterilised jar in the fridge.

5 For the kebabs, rub the harissa paste all over the lamb cubes, place in an airtight container and refrigerate overnight.

6 About 30 minutes before you are ready to braai, push the lamb onto bamboo skewers with the nectarines and mint leaves. Brush the nectarines with the 15ml (1 tbsp) olive oil and braai or grill, turning frequently until cooked to your liking, about 10 – 15 minutes for medium-rare. Serve hot.

Chicken thighs with lime juice and ginger

RECIPE BY **SUSAN GREIG** STYLING BY **ANNA MONTALI** PHOTOGRAPH BY **GRAEME BORCHERS**

Serves 6 **EASY** 35 mins + 2 hrs, to marinate

THE FLAVOUR COMBINATIONS

6 chicken thighs, with skin
juice of 4 limes
2 lemongrass sticks, thinly sliced
4 small red chillies, seeded and sliced
50ml fresh ginger, grated
4 spring onions, finely chopped
2 garlic cloves, finely chopped
45ml honey
5ml salt

HOW TO DO IT

1 Prepare the coals for the braai. Place the chicken pieces in a roasting tray and cut a few deep slashes into the skin and flesh.

2 Mix the remaining ingredients together. Pour the marinade over the chicken thighs, rubbing it into the slits. Cover and refrigerate for 2 hours, turning from time to time.

3 Place the thighs on the braai and cook until the chicken is golden, fragrant and cooked through, about 20 minutes. Serve hot.

23

Fettuccine served with baby marrow, peas and fresh herbs

RECIPE AND STYLING BY **ANNA MONTALI** PHOTOGRAPH BY **GRAEME BORCHERS**

Serves 4 **EASY** 20 mins

THE FLAVOUR COMBINATIONS

20ml olive oil
10ml butter
4 baby marrows, thickly sliced and blanched
50ml fresh peas, blanched
30ml fresh flat-leaf parsley, finely chopped
30ml fresh basil leaves, torn
250ml fresh cream
500g fettuccine
100g ricotta, crumbled

HOW TO DO IT

1 Heat the olive oil and butter in a pan and add the baby marrows, peas and herbs. Sauté until lightly coloured, about 2 minutes. Add the cream, cook and stir for a further 2 minutes.

2 Cook the pasta in plenty of salted boiling water until al dente. Remove and drain.

3 To serve, place the pasta in a serving dish and toss through the baby-marrow mixture. Top with the ricotta and serve hot.

COOK'S TIPS

To make this dish healthier, omit the butter and substitute the cream with yoghurt, but do not cook it. Simply mix it through after you have sautéed the vegetables and herbs. To make the sauce more decadent, combine the fresh cream with 100ml crème fraîche.

Rose-and-pistachio frozen nougat

RECIPE AND STYLING BY **QUENTIN SPICKERNELL** PHOTOGRAPH BY **MICHAEL LE GRANGE**

Serves 6 – 8 **EASY** 30 mins +
4 hrs or overnight, to freeze

THE FLAVOUR COMBINATIONS
**melted butter/sunflower oil,
to brush
3 egg whites
110g castor sugar
200ml fresh cream
rose water, to taste
75g Turkish dried apricots, chopped
75g pistachio nuts, roasted and
chopped + extra, to garnish
2,5ml (½ tsp) grapefruit zest + extra,
to garnish
100g fresh dates,
pitted and chopped
handful pomegranate rubies,
to garnish
small handful fresh mint leaves,
to garnish
icing sugar, to dust**

HOW TO DO IT

1 Line a 22cm x 8cm loaf tin with heavy-duty foil and brush lightly with some melted butter or sunflower oil. Line the tin with non-stick baking paper (this goes over the foil – so it is, in fact, a double lining) and leave a lip of paper hanging over the edges all around.

2 Place the egg whites and castor sugar in a heatproof bowl that fits snugly over a pot of gently simmering water (don't let the bottom of the bowl touch the water). Using an electric hand-held beater, whisk on a low speed until the mixture has reached 65°C on a sugar thermometer.

3 Tip the egg-white mixture into the bowl of an electric mixer with a whisk attachment and mix on high speed, 3 minutes. Reduce the speed to medium and keep whisking for a further 3 minutes. Reduce again to the slowest speed and whisk for a final 3 minutes or until the mixture reaches room temperature and looks thick and glossy.

4 In a separate bowl, whip the cream to soft peaks. Fold the whipped cream into the meringue, add a few drops of rose water to taste and fold in the fruit and nuts carefully.

5 Pour the mixture into the prepared loaf tin, smoothing the top so it's level, and cover with cling film. Place in the freezer for a minimum of 4 hours, but preferably overnight, until firm.

6 Just before serving, tip the frozen nougat out of the loaf tin and remove the baking paper. Using a sharp knife, cut into thick slices and serve immediately garnished with pomegranate rubies, mint leaves, pistachio nuts, grapefruit zest and dusted with icing sugar.

27

Blueberry-and-lavender cream tart

RECIPE AND STYLING BY **VICKI CLARKE** AND **NIKKI GASKELL** PHOTOGRAPH BY **ELSA YOUNG**

Serves 6 – 8 **EASY** 1 hr

THE FLAVOUR COMBINATIONS
400g roll puff pastry, defrosted
1 large egg, lightly beaten

LAVENDER CREAM
juice of 2 lemons
30ml (2 tbsp) lavender leaves, stripped
and slightly crushed
100g castor sugar
300ml fresh cream, lightly beaten
150g mascarpone
350g fresh blueberries
icing sugar, to dust (optional)

HOW TO DO IT

1 Preheat the oven to 210°C. Roll out the pastry on a floured surface to about 0,4cm thick and press it into a 29cm x 21cm rectangular tart tin. Trim the edges to leave about 0,5cm of pastry hanging over the lip of the tin. Prick the pastry base all over with a fork and freeze for 5 minutes.

2 Remove the pastry case from the freezer and blind-bake in the oven until golden, about 30 minutes. Remove from oven and leave to cool.

3 For the lavender cream, place the lemon juice, lavender leaves and castor sugar in a bowl, mix well and set aside for the sugar to dissolve. In a separate bowl, combine the cream and mascarpone. Strain the lemon mixture into the cream mixture and discard the lavender leaves. Whisk until the mixture is well combined and slightly thickened.

4 Spoon the lavender cream into the pastry case, cover with the berries, dust with icing sugar and serve.

This dessert can be made with a combination of summer berries, like blueberries, gooseberries, raspberries and strawberries, or with just one of these. The lavender adds a delicate scent to the dish. However, if lavender is not available, use 10ml (2 tbsp) vanilla essence or seeds from 2 vanilla pods instead.

This ice cream has
a slight crunch with
A DELIGHTFUL
HONEY FLAVOUR

Honey-and-amaretti-biscuit ice cream

RECIPE AND STYLING BY **LEILA SAFFARIAN** ASSISTED BY **NOMVUSELELO MNCUBE** PHOTOGRAPH BY **ROELENE PRINSLOO**

Makes 1 large tub **EASY** 20 mins + overnight to chill and 4 hrs, to freeze

THE FLAVOUR COMBINATIONS
60ml (¼ cup) honey + extra, to serve
500ml (2 cups) full-cream milk
500ml (2 cups) fresh cream
1 vanilla pod, split, seeded and seeds retained
6 large egg yolks
150g (¾ cup) sugar
150g amaretti biscuits, crushed
fresh nectarines, sliced, to serve

HOW TO DO IT

1 Place the honey, milk, cream, vanilla pod and seeds in a large saucepan and bring to a boil.

2 While the mixture is heating, combine the egg yolks and sugar in a bowl and whisk using an electric beater until the mixture is thick and pale, about 5 minutes.

3 Remove the milk mixture from the heat and gradually add to the egg yolks. Add slowly to prevent the eggs from curdling, mixing as you pour.

4 Return the mixture to the saucepan and stir over a low-medium heat until the mixture is thick enough to coat the back of a spoon. Pour the custard into a large bowl, cover with cling film and refrigerate overnight.

5 Prepare the ice-cream maker and strain the custard through a sieve, discarding the vanilla pod. Pour into the ice-cream maker and chill according to the manufacturer's instructions. Alternatively, if an ice-cream churner is not available, place the mixture in a freezer-proof container in the freezer until almost frozen but still fairly liquid. Whisk using an electric beater until creamy and return to the freezer until set.

6 When the ice cream is almost set, add half of the biscuits and mix through. Pour into a large freezer-safe container, cover and freeze for 4 hours or overnight.

7 Serve with the remaining biscuits, sliced nectarines and extra honey.

COOK'S TIPS
Save the used vanilla pod. Allow it to dry, then pop it into a container of sugar for a vanilla flavour. Use any seasonal fruit of your choice when serving the honey ice cream or replace the amaretti biscuits with crushed nuts.

Soft-centred chocolate mini cakes

RECIPE AND STYLING BY **ANNA MONTALI** PHOTOGRAPH BY **GRAEME WYLLIE**

Serves 6 **EASY** 10 mins

THE FLAVOUR COMBINATIONS
180g butter, at room temperature
300g good-quality dark chocolate
125g icing sugar, sifted + extra, to dust
80g cake flour, sifted
5 large eggs, lightly beaten

ice cream/fresh cream/mascarpone, to serve
puréed seasonal fruit, to serve (optional)

HOW TO DO IT
1 Preheat the oven to 200°C. Melt the butter and chocolate in a small pot and stir to combine well.

2 Mix the sugar and flour in a mixing bowl and fold in the eggs. Add the chocolate mixture and stir well.

3 Pour the batter into 6 greased ramekins, filling them three quarters of the way up, and bake in the oven, 7 minutes.

4 Dust with icing sugar and serve immediately with ice cream, fresh cream or mascarpone and, if desired, puréed seasonal fruit.

COOK'S TIPS
The cooking time is very important in order to achieve the liquid centre.

THE MONTH OF *February*

IT'S THE MONTH OF LOVE AND WE'VE GATHERED SOME OF OUR FINEST DISHES FOR THE PERFECT DINNER FOR TWO, A MEAL WITH GOOD FRIENDS OR A COSY NIGHT IN. EASY, TASTY AND FABULOUS TO LOOK AT, WHOEVER YOU'RE ENTERTAINING IS SURE TO LEAVE SATISFIED… AND SUPER-IMPRESSED

'Love you berry much' sorbet Champagne floats

RECIPE, STYLING AND PHOTOGRAPH BY **KATELYN WILLIAMS**

Serves 2 **EASY** 20 mins + freezing time

THE FLAVOUR COMBINATIONS
300g frozen mixed berries
100g castor sugar
2,5ml (½ tsp) vanilla extract
15ml (1 tbsp) vodka (optional)
juice of 1 lime
1 egg white
fresh blueberries, cherries or strawberries, frozen, to decorate
chilled Champagne, to top up

HOW TO DO IT

1 Place the mixed berries, sugar, vanilla, vodka (if desired) and lime juice in a blender and blitz until smooth. Add the egg white and briefly blend again. Pour into a freezer-safe container and freeze until almost firm, then blend again and return to the freezer until frozen.

2 Serve scoops of the sorbet in chilled Champagne coupes with the fruit and top up with the chilled bubbly.

Oysters with red onion, balsamic and coriander salsa

RECIPE AND STYLING BY **VICKI CLARKE** AND **NIKKI WEFELMEIER** PHOTOGRAPH BY **ELSA YOUNG**

Serves 6 **EASY** 15 mins

THE FLAVOUR COMBINATIONS
12 fresh oysters
5 red spring onions, finely chopped
50ml fresh coriander, finely chopped
45ml balsamic vinegar
30ml lime juice
2ml Tabasco
freshly ground black pepper, to taste

HOW TO DO IT

1 Shuck the oysters by inserting a very sharp, flat knife into them and twisting – better yet, ask your fishmonger to do this for you.

2 Place the remaining ingredients in a mixing bowl and stir well to combine.

3 Place a teaspoon of the mixture onto each oyster and serve immediately on crushed ice with a glass of good bubbly.

If chocolate is the
FOOD OF LOVE, THEN THIS
IS WITHOUT DOUBT
THE FOOD OF PASSION

Watermelon soup

RECIPE AND STYLING BY **REUBEN RIFFEL** PHOTOGRAPH BY **ROELENE PRINSLOO**

Serves 4 – 6 **EASY** 15 mins

THE FLAVOUR COMBINATIONS
1 watermelon, skinned, seeded and cubed
juice of 1 lemon
juice of 1 yuzu/30ml (2 tbsp) bottled yuzu juice (see Cook's tip) + extra, to drizzle
bunch fresh coriander + extra, to garnish
1 sweet melon, skinned, seeded and cubed
olive oil, to drizzle

HOW TO DO IT
1 Place half of the watermelon cubes in a food processor and blend with the lemon juice, yuzu juice and coriander until smooth.

2 Pour the soup into bowls and add a few cubes of watermelon and sweet melon.

3 Drizzle with the extra yuzu juice and a few drops of olive oil. Serve garnished with the extra coriander.

COOK'S TIP
Yuzu is a Japanese citrus fruit of about the same size as a naartjie, with the colour and texture of a rough lemon and a distinctive sour taste. The rind is often used to flavour Japanese fish- or noodle dishes. You can sometimes find fresh yuzu at Asian supermarkets. Alternatively, use the bottled juice, available at specialist grocers, or simply substitute with extra lemon juice.

Griddled aubergine with mozzarella, mint and pomegranate rubies

RECIPE AND STYLING BY **TRACY FOULKES** PHOTOGRAPH BY **NEIL CORDER**

Serves 6 **EASY** 30 mins

THE FLAVOUR COMBINATIONS
MARINADE
125ml extra-virgin olive oil
30ml ground cumin
1 garlic clove, crushed
sea salt and freshly ground
black pepper, to taste

3 aubergines,
cut into 1cm-thick slices
1 ball buffalo mozzarella,
torn into pieces
100g pomegranate rubies
50ml fresh mint leaves

HOW TO DO IT

1 Heat a griddle plan over high heat. Combine the marinade ingredients and baste the aubergine slices well. Allow to marinate for about 5 minutes.

2 When the griddle pan is smoking hot, chargrill the marinated aubergine slices on each side until char lines appear.

3 Arrange the chargrilled aubergine slices on a serving platter with the torn mozzarella, pomegranate rubies and mint scattered on top. Drizzle with the remaining marinade and serve.

COOK'S TIP
Pomegranate rubies are subject to availability, so leave them out if you can't find them.

Rare beef salad with five-spice poached apples

RECIPE AND STYLING BY **ANKE ROUX** PHOTOGRAPH BY **NEIL CORDER**

Serves 4 – 6 **EASY** 35 mins

THE FLAVOUR COMBINATIONS
300g aged fillet steak
10ml olive oil + extra, to drizzle
20ml freshly ground black pepper

POACHING LIQUID
500ml red wine
150g sugar
2 star anise
1 cinnamon stick, broken
15ml fennel seeds
5 cloves
6 peppercorns
5ml salt

4 – 6 baby apples, peeled
1 bunch fresh wild rocket
2 rounds feta

HOW TO DO IT

1 Rub the meat with the olive oil and season on all sides with the pepper.

2 Heat a griddle pan to smoking point and quickly sear the meat on all sides. Allow to rest and then cut into thin slices.

3 Mix all of the poaching-liquid ingredients in a saucepan and bring to a boil. Cook for 15 minutes, add the apples and cook for 5 minutes. Turn off heat and allow the apples to cool in the liquid.

4 Arrange the rocket, feta, apples and fillet slices on a platter.

5 Dress the salad with a drizzle of olive oil and a couple of tablespoons of the poaching liquid, and serve.

Prawn-and-chilli risotto

RECIPE AND STYLING BY **ANNA MONTALI** PHOTOGRAPH BY **GRAEME BORCHERS**

Serves 4 **EASY** 40 mins

THE FLAVOUR COMBINATIONS
40ml butter
20ml (4 tsp) olive oil
1 onion, finely chopped
1 garlic clove, finely chopped
200g carnaroli/arborio rice
1,2 litres good-quality fish stock, hot
500g prawns, cleaned and shelled
2 fresh green chillies,
seeded and finely chopped
salt and freshly ground
black pepper, to taste
250ml (1 cup) fresh cream
fresh flat-leaf parsley, finely
chopped, to garnish

HOW TO DO IT

1 Heat the butter and olive oil in a large frying pan and sauté the onion and garlic for 2 minutes.

2 Add the rice and stir to combine with the onion-and-garlic mixture. Slowly add the fish stock one ladleful at a time, making sure that the liquid has been absorbed before adding the next ladleful. Stir until all of the stock has been used and the rice is al dente.

3 Add the prawns and chillies, stir through the risotto and cook until the prawns are heated through, 5 – 10 minutes. Season.

4 Add the cream and heat through. Sprinkle with the chopped parsley and serve hot.

46

Rolled smoked springbok carpaccio with asparagus and caprino

RECIPE AND STYLING BY **PETER ROSE** PHOTOGRAPH BY **BRUCE TUCK**

Serves 4 as starter **EASY** 15 mins

THE FLAVOUR COMBINATIONS
12 – 20 green asparagus
160g springbok carpaccio
100g caprino (goat's cheese), shaved
micro beetroot shoots, to serve
olive oil, to serve
balsamic reduction, to serve
salt and freshly ground
black pepper, to taste

HOW TO DO IT

1 Trim the green asparagus and cook in boiling water until al dente, 4 – 5 minutes. Plunge into cold water and drain.

2 Roll the cooled asparagus spears in slices of carpaccio and cover with caprino shavings.

3 To serve, garnish with beetroot shoots, drizzle over olive oil and balsamic reduction, and season.

COOK'S TIPS
Beef or kudu carpaccio works just as well as springbok. Leave hard cheeses like Parmesan, pecorino or caprino uncovered in the fridge for a few hours to harden even more before shaving or grating.

Pork belly with teriyaki glaze and scallop butter

RECIPE AND STYLING BY **JACQUES ERASMUS** PHOTOGRAPH BY **MYBURGH DU PLESSIS**

Serves 6 **EASY** 2 hrs

THE FLAVOUR COMBINATIONS
1kg pork belly
white pepper, to taste

TERIYAKI GLAZE
200ml teriyaki sauce
60ml (¼ cup) soft brown sugar
2cm fresh ginger, bruised

SCALLOP BUTTER
50g scallop roe
125g butter
2,5ml (½ tsp) lemon zest
2,5ml (½ tsp) chilli flakes + extra,
to garnish

fresh pea shoots, to garnish

HOW TO DO IT

1 Preheat the oven to 160°C. Score the pork belly in a diamond pattern on the skin side, place in a roasting tray, sprinkle with white pepper and bake until the skin is crisp and the meat is tender, 1 hour and 45 minutes. Remove from oven and allow to cool a little before cutting into slices.

2 For the teriyaki glaze, place the teriyaki sauce with the sugar and ginger in a saucepan over medium heat and reduce by half.

3 For the scallop butter, combine the scallop roe, butter, lemon zest and chilli flakes in a food processor and blend until you have a smooth compound butter.

4 Heat the cooled pork belly slices in the oven until hot. Place a slice of pork belly on each serving plate and spoon over 15ml (1 tbsp) of the teriyaki glaze. Finish with a dollop of the scallop butter, sprinkle with chilli flakes and garnish with pea shoots.

Potato-and-prosciutto tart

RECIPE BY **SUE GREIG** STYLING BY **ANNA MONTALI** PHOTOGRAPH BY **GRAEME BORCHERS**

Serves 4 **EASY** 40 mins

THE FLAVOUR COMBINATIONS
400g roll puff pastry, defrosted
6 new potatoes, thinly sliced
30ml (2 tbsp) olive oil
salt and freshly ground
black pepper, to taste
8 slices prosciutto, torn
2 garlic cloves, sliced
1 jumbo egg, lightly beaten
50g (½ cup) Parmesan, grated

DRESSING
110g (½ cup) good-quality
mayonnaise
15ml (1 tbsp) Parmesan, grated
15ml (1 tbsp) lemon juice

HOW TO DO IT

1 Preheat the oven to 200°C and line a 23cm Swiss-roll tin with baking paper.

2 Roll out the pastry on a lightly floured work surface and line the tin. Score a 1cm border around the edge of the pastry with a sharp knife.

3 Place the potato slices and oil in a bowl, season and toss to combine. Layer the potato mixture, prosciutto and garlic on the pastry and brush the edges of the pastry with the egg.

4 Bake until the pastry is golden and the potato is tender, about 20 – 25 minutes.

5 Remove from oven, slide the tart out of the tin carefully and sprinkle with the 50g (½ cup) grated Parmesan.

6 For the dressing, combine all of the ingredients and stir well. Set aside until ready to be served, dolloped on top of the tart.

Chewy coconut meringues with caramelised plums

RECIPE AND STYLING BY **ANKE ROUX** PHOTOGRAPH BY **RIANA VOGEL**

Serves 6 **EASY** 45 mins

THE FLAVOUR COMBINATIONS
2 egg whites
5ml vanilla essence
200g sugar
10ml desiccated coconut
80g butter
6 plums, stoned and halved
100g sugar
250ml crème fraîche

HOW TO DO IT

1 Preheat the oven to 150°C. Using an electric mixer, beat the egg whites until soft-peak stage. Add the vanilla and 15ml of the 200g sugar at a time until the mixture forms stiff peaks.

2 Spoon the meringue mixture onto a greased baking sheet and shape into six little nests. Scatter the coconut over and bake for 25 – 30 minutes. Remove from oven and set aside until needed.

3 Melt the butter in a pan over medium heat and fry the plums for 1 minute before adding the 100g sugar. Allow the plums to cook in the sugary sauce for a few minutes. Remove and set aside.

4 Spoon a generous dollop of crème fraîche into the centre of each meringue nest and top with a caramelised plum. Drizzle a little sauce over and serve immediately.

54

These make a
GREAT
IMPRESSION

Lush and lovely chocolate-cherry cake

RECIPE AND STYLING BY **SARAH DALL** PHOTOGRAPH BY **CHRISTOPH HEIERLI**

Serves 6 – 8 **EASY** 60 mins

THE FLAVOUR COMBINATIONS
50ml cocoa
80ml (¹/₃ cup) boiling water
225g castor sugar
225g unsalted butter
3 extra-large eggs
225g self-raising flour
100ml buttermilk
350g fresh cherries, half pitted,
half left whole

GANACHE
250ml (1 cup) fresh cream
200g good-quality dark chocolate,
roughly chopped

HOW TO DO IT

1 Preheat the oven to 180°C. Line the base of two 20cm-round cake tins and grease the sides.

2 Mix together the cocoa and boiling water until smooth.

3 Beat the sugar and butter until thickened, pale and fluffy. Add the eggs one at a time, whisking continuously.

4 Fold through the cocoa mixture, sifted flour and buttermilk. Pour into the prepared tins and bake until the cake sponges are well risen and cooked through, 20 – 25 minutes. A skewer inserted into the centre of the sponges should come out clean.

5 Remove from oven and set aside to cool in the tins. Turn out onto a wire cooling rack.

6 For the ganache, place the cream in a pot and heat, but do not let it simmer. Remove from heat and whisk in the chocolate. Pour into a large bowl and use an electric whisk to thicken the ganache. Chill in the fridge for 30 minutes.

7 Spread the ganache over the top of each sponge. Add the pitted cherries to the ganache on the bottom sponge. Top the second sponge with the whole cherries, sandwich together and serve.

Peanut-butter chocolate fondants

RECIPE AND STYLING BY **SARAH DALL** PHOTOGRAPH BY **CHRISTOPH HEIERLI**

Serves 8 **EASY** 30 mins

THE FLAVOUR COMBINATIONS
180g good-quality dark chocolate
200g butter, softened
100g castor sugar
4 extra-large eggs
4 extra-large yolks
50g cake flour
130g peanut butter

HOW TO DO IT

1 Preheat the oven to 180°C. Grease and line the base of 8 ramekins and arrange on a baking sheet.

2 Place the chocolate in a glass bowl and melt over a double boiler. (Do not allow the bowl to touch the water.)

3 Cream the butter and sugar together until thickened, pale and fluffy. Add the eggs and egg yolks, one at a time, whisking continuously after each addition. Slowly add the melted chocolate and mix well. Sift the flour and fold into the mixture.

4 Half-fill the ramekins by spooning 15ml (1 tbsp) peanut butter in the centre of each and covering with the chocolate mixture. Make sure the ramekins are only three quarters full. Bake in the oven until well risen, 12 – 15 minutes. Remove from oven and allow to rest, 2 minutes. Loosen the edges, turn out onto a plate immediately and serve.

58

THE MONTH OF *March*

SOAK UP THE LAST OF BALMY SUMMER DAYS AND EVENINGS WITH
ONLY THE BEST FARE AND GREAT COMPANY. BEFORE IT GETS TOO
COLD, ENJOY LAZY ALFRESCO LUNCHES, TRYING OUT EVERYTHING
FROM FAMILY PIZZA BOARDS AND SAUCY SEAFOOD STACKS TO TASTY
MEZE AND SWOON-WORTHY TARTS – ALL GREAT FOR SHARING!

Melon caipirinhas

RECIPE BY **JULES MERCER** STYLING BY **TARA SLOGGETT** PHOTOGRAPH BY **TOBY MURPHY**

Makes 6 **EASY** 10 mins +
2 – 4 hrs, to soak

THE FLAVOUR COMBINATIONS
1 orange cantaloupe melon,
thinly sliced
300ml white rum
85g castor sugar
juice of 2 large lemons

HOW TO DO IT

1 Lay the melon in a flat rectangular-shaped container and drizzle with the rum. Cover and refrigerate for 2 – 4 hours so the melon can soak up the alcohol.

2 In a cocktail shaker, mix the sugar with the lemon juice and shake until dissolved. Add the rum from the melons and shake to mix.

3 Divide the mixture among tall glasses and add a few slices of the melon to each glass. Top with crushed ice and use the melon slices as swizzle sticks.

These delicious fruits burst with flavour during
the summer months but if you can't find a cantaloupe,
any sweet melon will do.

Meze stack

RECIPE AND STYLING BY **ANNA MONTALI** ASSISTED BY **NOMVUSELELO MNCUBE** PHOTOGRAPH BY **GRAEME BORCHERS**

Serves 4 – 6 **EASY** 45 mins

THE FLAVOUR COMBINATIONS
MEATBALLS
45ml (3 tbsp) butter
30ml (2 tbsp) olive oil
2 garlic cloves, finely chopped
1 onion, finely chopped
560g beef mince
salt and freshly ground black
pepper, to taste
1 large egg
180g fresh breadcrumbs
60ml (¼ cup) fresh flat-leaf parsley,
finely chopped
30ml (2 tbsp) dried oregano
zest of 1 lemon
cake flour, to coat
vegetable oil, to deep-fry

FETA
1 large egg
45ml (3 tbsp) sesame oil
225g traditional feta rounds
55g (¹/₃ cup) sesame seeds
oil, to fry

HOW TO DO IT

1 To make the meatballs, heat the butter and olive oil in a frying pan and gently sauté the garlic and onion for a few minutes.

2 Place the mince in a bowl and season. Add the garlic mixture from the pan together with the egg, breadcrumbs, parsley, oregano and lemon zest and mix to combine well.

3 Wet your hands and roll the mixture into small meatballs about the size of a large marble, rolling them in the flour to coat lightly.

4 Heat the vegetable oil in a deep-fryer or large pot to 180°C and deep-fry the meatballs until golden, 2 – 3 minutes. Drain on paper towel and keep warm.

5 For the feta, whisk the egg and sesame oil well together. Place the feta in the egg mixture and leave to soak for a few minutes.

6 Coat the feta in the sesame seeds and refrigerate for 5 minutes.

7 Heat the oil and pan-fry the feta until golden and slightly soft on the inside, 5 – 8 minutes.

8 Drain on paper towel and serve warm alongside the meatballs and additions of your choice.

64

Add anything with a Mediterranean flavour to these savoury stacks: olives, marinated peppers, pickled artichokes, roasted tomatoes, dolmades, dips, breads… whatever you fancy.

Grilled polenta squares with vine tomatoes, cucumber and feta

RECIPE AND STYLING BY **ILLANIQUE VAN ASWEGEN** PHOTOGRAPH BY **ADEL FERREIRA**

Serves 4 as a starter **EASY** 45 mins + setting time

THE FLAVOUR COMBINATIONS

1L water
5ml (1 tsp) salt
190g (1 cup) polenta
50g (½ cup) Parmesan, grated
4 stalks of vine tomatoes
15ml (1 tbsp) olive oil + extra, to serve
150g (¹/₃ cup) basil pesto
100g (½ cup) Danish feta, cubed
8 cucumber ribbons
150g (½ cup) tin borlotti beans, rinsed and drained
a few sprigs of watercress

HOW TO DO IT

1 Preheat the oven grill to high. Line a shallow 30cm x 25cm baking dish with cling film, allowing the plastic to hang over the sides of the dish.

2 Bring the water and salt to a boil. Whisk in the polenta and lower the heat to allow the polenta to gently simmer, 15 minutes. Keep an eye on it to make sure it doesn't burn at the bottom of the pot.

3 Stir in the Parmesan and pour the polenta into the lined dish. Allow to set until firm, about 2 hours.

4 Place the tomatoes in an oven tray and drizzle with the oil. Grill until blistered and tender, 6 – 8 minutes.

5 Place a griddle pan over medium-high heat. Slice the polenta into starter-size squares and fry on both sides. Alternatively, use a normal frying pan and cook the polenta in some butter until golden.

6 Add a generous smear of pesto to the polenta and top with the tomatoes, feta, cucumber ribbons, beans and watercress. Add a drizzle of the extra oil just before serving.

COOK'S TIP
You can make the polenta ahead of time up until the end of step 3 and keep in a sealed container in the fridge for up to 2 days. Grill just before serving.

Chargrilled broccoli with chilli and garlic

RECIPE BY **SUE GREIG** STYLING BY **ANNA MONTALI** PHOTOGRAPH BY **GRAEME BORCHERS**

Serves 4 **EASY** 20 mins

THE FLAVOUR COMBINATIONS
500g broccoli, separated into florets
120ml olive oil
sea salt and freshly ground black
pepper, to taste
4 garlic cloves, thinly sliced
2 mild red chillies,
seeded and thinly sliced
4 anchovy fillets
flaked almonds, to garnish

HOW TO DO IT

1 Blanch the broccoli in boiling water for 2 minutes. Plunge into ice-cold water, drain and leave to dry. Toss the broccoli in a bowl with 45ml (3 tbsp) of the olive oil. Season.

2 Heat a griddle pan over high heat and fry the broccoli in batches, turning it frequently to get light chargrill marks all over. Transfer the broccoli to a heatproof bowl and keep warm.

3 Combine the remaining olive oil, garlic, chillies and anchovies in a frying pan. Cook over medium heat until the garlic turns golden brown. Be careful not to overcook and burn the garlic.

4 Pour the garlic mixture over the broccoli and toss through. Check the seasoning, garnish with almonds and serve warm.

Lemon-and-caper chicken fillets

RECIPE AND STYLING BY **LEILA SAFFARIAN** ASSISTED BY **NOMVUSELELO MNCUBE** PHOTOGRAPH BY **GRAEME WYLLIE**

Serves 4 – 6 **EASY** 35 mins

THE FLAVOUR COMBINATIONS
6 skinless chicken breasts
sea salt and freshly ground black
pepper, to taste
cake flour, to dust
60ml (¼ cup) olive oil
45ml (3 tbsp) capers,
drained and chopped
juice and zest of 1 large lemon
large handful of fresh flat-leaf
parsley, roughly chopped
tagliatelle pasta, cooked, to serve
lemon wedges, to serve

HOW TO DO IT

1 Cut the chicken breasts in half lengthways and place on a wooden board between two sheets of cling film. Using a meat mallet, lightly flatten the breasts until fairly thin. Season.

2 Dust the chicken fillets with flour, shaking off the excess. Heat 30ml (2 tbsp) of the oil in a large non-stick frying pan over medium heat and fry the chicken in batches on both sides until golden, about 3 – 4 minutes per side. Remove from pan and set aside until needed.

3 Add the remaining oil to the same pan, together with the capers and lemon zest, and fry over medium heat for 1 minute.

4 Return the chicken fillets to the pan and add the lemon juice. Fry for a further 2 – 3 minutes.

5 Adjust the seasoning and scatter with parsley. Serve with tagliatelle and lemon wedges.

COOK'S TIP
For a leaner option, halve the amount of olive oil for frying and serve with a green salad instead of pasta.

Carrot, crab and avocado salad

RECIPE AND STYLING BY **JACQUES ERASMUS** PHOTOGRAPH BY **MYBURGH DU PLESSIS**

Serves 4 as a starter **EASY** 20 mins

THE FLAVOUR COMBINATIONS
½ onion, chopped
1 garlic clove
15ml (1 tbsp) coriander seeds, crushed
25ml sugar
25ml white wine vinegar
50ml olive oil
2,5ml (½ tsp) dried chilli flakes
400g crab meat, cooked and drained
25ml mascarpone
25ml good-quality mayonnaise
5ml (1 tsp) fresh lemon juice
2 avocados, peeled and lightly mashed
4 – 5 medium carrots, peeled and finely grated
shaved carrots, to serve
onion sprouts, to serve

HOW TO DO IT

1 Dry-fry the onion in a pan over medium heat, 2 – 3 minutes.

2 Add the garlic, coriander seeds, sugar, vinegar, olive oil and chilli flakes. Bring to a boil and remove from heat.

3 Combine the crab meat, mascarpone, mayonnaise and lemon juice, and mix well.

4 Place spoonfuls of the crab mixture, avocado and grated carrots in a 15cm ring mould on a plate and press down lightly.

5 Remove the mould, spoon over the dressing and top with the shaved carrots and onion sprouts. Serve immediately.

Seafood platters
ARE IDEAL FOR
S H A R I N G

Saucy seafood platter

RECIPE AND STYLING BY **LEILA SAFFARIAN** ASSISTED BY **NOMVUSELELO MNCUBE** PHOTOGRAPH BY **GRAEME WYLLIE**

Serves 4 – 6 **EASY** 50 mins

THE FLAVOUR COMBINATIONS
TOMATO SAUCE
30ml (2 tbsp) olive oil
1 small onion, finely chopped
2 garlic cloves, chopped
2 x 410g tins chopped tomatoes
5ml (1 tsp) dried oregano
2,5ml (½ tsp) dried chilli flakes (optional)
5ml (1 tsp) sugar
60ml (¼ cup) water

SEAFOOD
sea salt and freshly ground black pepper, to taste
12 whole tiger prawns, cleaned
200g fresh calamari tubes and tentacles, cleaned
fresh flat-leaf parsley, roughly chopped, to serve
fresh crusty bread, to serve
lemon wedges, to serve

HOW TO DO IT

1 For the tomato sauce, heat the oil in a medium saucepan over medium heat and gently fry the onion until golden. Add the garlic, tinned tomatoes, oregano, chilli flakes, sugar and water, and season well. Let the sauce cook for 15 – 20 minutes over low-medium heat until reduced and thick and chunky. Adjust seasoning and set aside.

2 Transfer the sauce to a large non-stick frying pan or shallow casserole dish that can be used on a stovetop. Warm over medium heat and add the prawns. Cover with a lid and cook for 5 minutes. Add the calamari and cover again with the lid. Cook for a further 5 minutes or until the prawns have turned pink and the calamari is cooked.

3 Adjust the seasoning and scatter parsley over before serving with fresh crusty bread and lemon wedges.

COOK'S TIP
You can add mussels and any type of sustainable fish to this platter – remember to check the SASSI website at wwfsassi.co.za for sustainable (Green List) fish varieties.

Lamb racks with broad beans and roasted veggies

RECIPE BY **KAREN SHORT** STYLING BY **CLIVE JOHNSON** AND **LOUISE THOMAS** PHOTOGRAPH BY **GRAEME WYLLIE**

Serves 4 **EASY** 40 mins

THE FLAVOUR COMBINATIONS
6 baby marrows, sliced diagonally
1 medium butternut, peeled and cut into cubes
2 small red onions, peeled and cut into thin wedges
2 garlic cloves, peeled and crushed
45ml (3 tbsp) olive oil
salt and freshly ground black pepper, to taste
16 cherry tomatoes
4 x 300g lamb racks (2 cutlets per person)
300g frozen or fresh broad beans
zest of 1 lemon
30ml (2 tbsp) fresh mint, chopped, plus whole sprigs to garnish

HOW TO DO IT

1 Preheat the oven to 180°C. Place the baby marrows, butternut, red onions and garlic in a roasting pan. Drizzle with the oil and season. Roast for about 30 minutes, adding the tomatoes during the last 5 minutes.

2 Increase the oven temperature to 200°C. Seal the lamb by placing the racks fat-side down in a hot pan or on a griddle. Allow to cool, rub salt into the fat and place the racks in a baking tray. Roast for 15 – 20 minutes for medium-rare. Cover and rest for 10 minutes.

3 Boil the broad beans in salted water, 2 – 3 minutes. Cool in a colander under cold running water, then drain. Make a slit in the top of each bean and remove the outer skin.

4 Add the beans, lemon zest and chopped mint to the roasted vegetables and stir gently.

5 Serve the lamb with the vegetables, garnished with mint sprigs.

Broad-bean, asparagus and smoked-salmon pasta

RECIPE BY **KAREN SHORT** STYLING BY **CLIVE JOHNSON** AND **LOUISE THOMAS** PHOTOGRAPH BY **GRAEME WYLLIE**

Serves 4 **EASY** 30 mins

THE FLAVOUR COMBINATIONS
30ml (2 tbsp) butter
6 spring onions, chopped
90ml dry white wine
200g crème fraîche
salt and freshly ground black pepper, to taste
30ml (2 tbsp) fresh dill, finely chopped
juice of ½ lemon
300g fresh or frozen broad beans
350g spaghetti
200g fresh asparagus, trimmed and chopped
180g smoked salmon, cut into small pieces

HOW TO DO IT

1 Melt the butter in a pan over medium heat and fry half of the spring onions until soft, about 1 minute.

2 Add the wine and boil until reduced to about 30ml (2 tbsp). Stir in the crème fraîche and season well. Bring to a boil and simmer until slightly thickened, 2 – 3 minutes. Stir in the dill and lemon juice. Set aside.

3 Boil the broad beans in salted water for 2 – 3 minutes. Cool in a colander under cold running water and drain. Make a slit in the top of each bean and remove the outer skin.

4 Cook the spaghetti in plenty of salted boiling water until al dente, adding the asparagus 3 minutes before the end of the cooking time. Drain the pasta and asparagus, reserving a little of the cooking water.

5 Toss the hot pasta and asparagus with the beans, salmon and crème fraîche sauce. If necessary, thin with a little of the reserved cooking water and adjust the seasoning.

6 Serve the pasta hot, garnished with the remaining spring onions.

79

Family pizza boards

RECIPE AND STYLING BY **LEILA SAFFARIAN** ASSISTED BY **NOMVUSELELO MNCUBE** PHOTOGRAPH BY **GRAEME WYLLIE**

Makes 2 pizzas **EASY** 45 mins +
35 mins, to rise

THE FLAVOUR COMBINATIONS
DOUGH
1kg cake flour
10g sachet instant dry yeast
5ml (1 tsp) salt
15ml (1 tbsp) sugar
45ml (3 tbsp) olive oil
625ml (2½ cups) lukewarm water

TOPPINGS
passata or tomato sauce
prosciutto
mozzarella, sliced
sun-dried tomatoes
portobellini mushrooms, sliced
selection of fresh herbs (basil,
oregano, rocket and sage)
olive oil, to drizzle
sea salt and freshly ground black
pepper, to taste
Parmesan, grated

HOW TO DO IT

1 For the dough, combine all of the dry ingredients in a large bowl and make a well in the centre. Pour the oil and half of the water into the well and start pulling flour in from the sides of the bowl. Add the remaining water to form a fairly sticky dough.

2 Turn the dough out onto a floured work surface and knead well until the dough becomes smooth and elastic, about 10 minutes.

3 Place the dough in a lightly oiled bowl and cover with a tea towel. Allow to rise in a warm place until doubled in size, about 35 minutes.

4 Preheat the oven to 220°C. Roll the dough out thinly and place on baking sheets. Spread with passata or tomato sauce and top with your choice of toppings. Drizzle with oil and season.

5 Bake in the preheated oven until crisp and golden, 10 – 12 minutes.

COOK'S TIPS
Pizza isn't necessarily bad. To reduce your carb intake, roll the dough out as thinly as possible. Using a small amount of low-fat, grated mozzarella helps with portion control.

Gluten-free chocolate torte

RECIPE BY **STEFAN PREDORF** AND **KATELYNNE WOOLDRIDGE** STYLING BY **TARYNE JAKOBI** PHOTOGRAPH BY **GRAEME WYLLIE**

Serves 8 – 10 **EASY** 90 mins

THE FLAVOUR COMBINATIONS
6 extra-large eggs, separated
150g castor sugar
250g 55% dark chocolate
120g salted butter
30g unsalted almonds, ground

GANACHE
coffee bean, to infuse
150ml fresh cream
150g Belgian dark chocolate,
roughly chopped

GARNISH
375g strawberries, sliced
20g Belgian white chocolate, melted

HOW TO DO IT

1 Preheat the oven to 140°C and line a 25cm-round cake tin with baking paper.

2 Beat the egg yolks and sugar until pale and fluffy.

3 Melt the 250g 55% dark chocolate and butter in a pot over low heat until smooth and shiny.

4 Add the melted chocolate mixture to the beaten egg yolks.

5 Beat the egg whites to stiff peaks and gently fold into the chocolate mixture. Fold in the ground almonds, then pour into the prepared tin and bake in the preheated oven, 40 minutes.

6 For the ganache, place the coffee bean in the cream and warm over a double boiler (do not allow the water to touch the bottom of the bowl). Strain the coffee bean, add the cream to the 150g Belgian dark chocolate, and stir until smooth and shiny.

7 To serve, top the cooled torte with the ganache and decorate with the strawberries and melted white chocolate.

83

Watermelon-and-vodka ices

RECIPE BY **JULES MERCER** STYLING BY **TARA SLOGGETT** PHOTOGRAPH BY **TOBY MURPHY**

Makes 8 **EASY** 15 mins +
2 – 3 hrs, to set

THE FLAVOUR COMBINATIONS
½ **watermelon, peeled and chopped**
500ml (2 cups) watermelon juice
60ml (¼ cup) vodka or more, to taste

HOW TO DO IT

1 In a blender, blitz the watermelon until smooth, then pour through a sieve into a measuring jug to make 500ml (2 cups). Stir in the vodka.

2 Pour into 30ml shot glasses and place in the freezer. Just as the ices are beginning to set, after about 1½ hours, place wooden lolly sticks in the glasses.

3 Allow to freeze for 2 – 3 hours until completely set.

4 Remove from the freezer and give the sticks a good turn – the ices should slip out easily. Serve in an ice bucket filled with ice cubes so the ices last a little longer.

Arguably the most refreshing of fruits for lazy summer afternoons, watermelon pairs incredibly well with vodka. Add some fresh mint leaves to the recipe if you fancy.

THE MONTH OF *April*

IT'S A MONTH TO CELEBRATE HEARTY, AUTUMN DISHES, AS WELL AS TRADITIONAL EASTER TREATS, SO GATHER YOUR LOVED ONES AND COOK UP A FEAST THAT WILL EASE YOU INTO WINTER

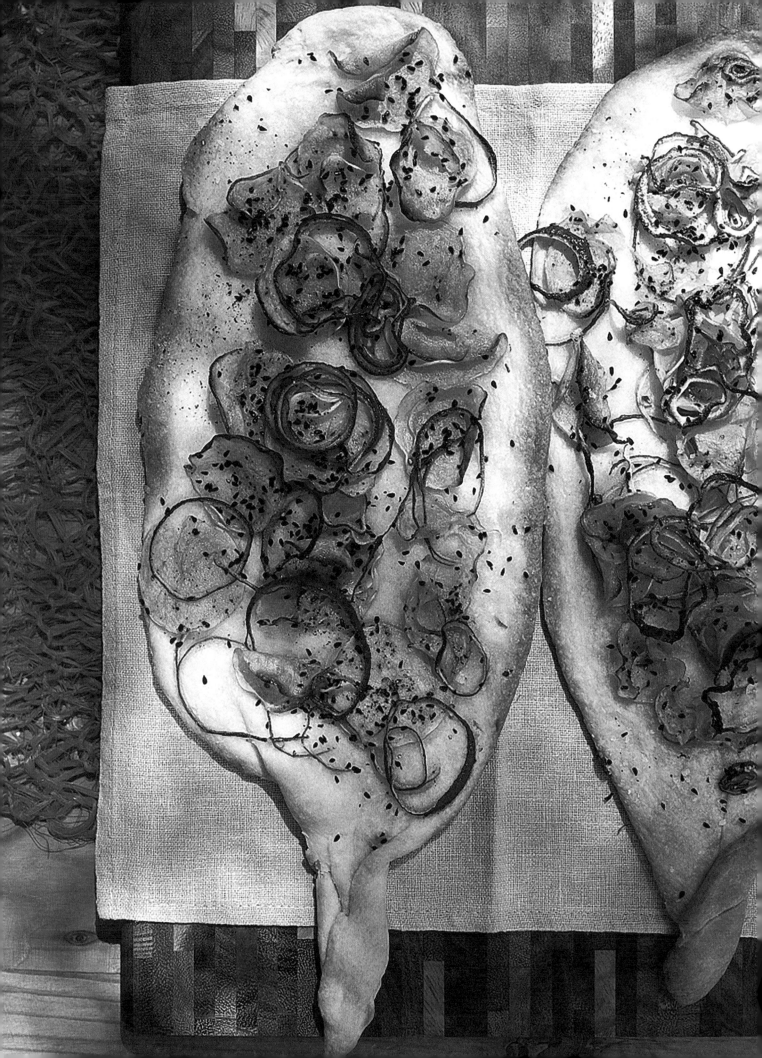

Butternut-and-onion flatbreads

RECIPE AND STYLING BY **ANKE ROUX** PHOTOGRAPH BY **NEIL CORDER**

Serves 8 **EASY** 30 mins +
2 hrs, to prove

THE FLAVOUR COMBINATIONS
2 x 10g sachets instant dry yeast
200ml warm milk
480g cake flour
15ml salt
150ml olive oil

TOPPING
1 butternut, shaved into rounds
1 red onion, finely sliced into rounds
olive oil, to drizzle
30ml onion seeds
salt and freshly ground black
pepper, to taste

HOW TO DO IT

1 Add the yeast to the warm milk and allow to stand for 15 minutes until frothy.

2 Sift together the flour and salt. Add the milk mixture and the 150ml olive oil. Mix well and knead until the dough is smooth and elastic, about 10 minutes – the dough should be quite stiff.

3 Place the dough in an oiled bowl, cover with cling film and allow to stand in a warm place to rise until doubled in size, about 2 hours.

4 When the dough has doubled in size, knock back and divide into four large or eight smaller balls. Roll each ball into an oval shape and twist one end to form a 'handle'. Place four baking trays in the oven and preheat it to 230°C.

5 Top each flatbread with some of the shaved butternut and onion, a drizzle of olive oil and a scattering of onion seeds. Season.

6 Bake on the preheated trays until crispy and golden, about 10 minutes. Serve hot.

COOK'S TIP
If you are pressed for time, use ready-made naan bread instead of making the flatbreads from scratch.

Sesame-and-Parmesan green beans

RECIPE AND STYLING BY **LEILA SAFFARIAN** ASSISTED BY **NOMVUSELELO MNCUBE** PHOTOGRAPH BY **ROELENE PRINSLOO**

Serves 4 EASY 20 mins

THE FLAVOUR COMBINATIONS
500g green beans, trimmed
45ml (3 tbsp) olive oil
juice of 2 limes
sea salt and freshly ground black
pepper, to taste
1 small red chilli, seeded and
finely chopped
60ml (¼ cup) sesame seeds, toasted
100g unsalted almonds,
roughly chopped
100g Parmesan, grated

HOW TO DO IT
1 Bring a large pot of salted water to a boil. Add the beans and cook for 3 minutes. Drain and refresh in ice-cold water.

2 Drain the beans and combine in a large mixing bowl with the oil, lime juice, seasoning, chilli, sesame seeds, almonds and Parmesan.

3 Combine well and spoon into serving bowls.

COOK'S TIP
These beans are great served with a zesty piece of fresh, grilled linefish.

The cinnamon and nuts make for a delicately spiced and crunchy topping on the tender squash.

Hubbard squash slices with a cinnamon-and-nut crust

RECIPE AND STYLING BY **ILLANIQUE VAN ASWEGEN** PHOTOGRAPH BY **ADEL FERREIRA**

Makes 8 **EASY** 60 mins

THE FLAVOUR COMBINATIONS
olive oil, to drizzle
800g (about 8) slices hubbard
squash, cut to a thickness of
about 2cm
salt and freshly ground black
pepper, to taste
30ml (2 tbsp) brown sugar
5ml (1 tsp) ground cinnamon
7,5ml (1½ tsp) fresh thyme,
finely chopped
25g cashews, finely chopped
25g shelled pistachios,
finely chopped
25g ginger biscuits, finely crushed
100g feta, to serve
handful fresh basil leaves, to garnish

HOW TO DO IT

1 Preheat the oven to 200°C. Lightly grease a large baking tray with olive oil.

2 Place the squash on the tray, drizzle lightly with olive oil, season to taste and roast, 30 minutes.

3 Stir the sugar, cinnamon, thyme, cashews, pistachios and biscuits together. Remove the squash from the oven, sprinkle with the crust mixture and roast for a further 15 minutes.

4 To serve, crumble over some feta and garnish with basil leaves.

COOK'S TIP
This sweet squash dish is the perfect addition to a Sunday lunch of roasted meat and veggies.

Autumn salad with deep-fried chevin

RECIPE AND STYLING BY **VICKIE DE BEER** ASSISTED BY **JANA VAN SITTERT** AND **INEMARI RABIE** PHOTOGRAPH BY **LEE MALAN**

Serves 4 **EASY** 20 mins

THE FLAVOUR COMBINATIONS
DRESSING
80ml (¹/₃ cup) olive oil
45ml (3 tbsp) balsamic vinegar
5ml (1 tsp) wholegrain mustard
5ml (1 tsp) honey
salt and freshly ground
black pepper, to taste

SALAD
20g (2 tbsp) butter
15ml (1 tbsp) honey
8 sprigs of thyme, leaves only
6 – 8 heirloom baby carrots, halved
100g walnuts
handful fresh rocket, to serve
handful mixed salad leaves (radicchio,
Swiss chard), to serve
250ml (1 cup) cooked beetroot,
cut into wedges, to serve
2 red apples, cored and
thinly sliced, to serve

CHEVIN
3 x 100g rolls chevin
40g flour
1 large egg, lightly beaten
35g (½ cup) fresh breadcrumbs
canola oil, to shallow-fry

HOW TO DO IT

1 Combine all of the ingredients for the dressing and set aside.

2 For the salad, heat the butter and honey in a small saucepan over medium heat. Add the thyme, carrots and walnuts, and fry until tender but not too soft. Remove from heat and set aside.

3 Slice the chevin rolls into 12 discs. Dip each piece in a little flour, shaking off the excess. Coat with the egg and then roll in the breadcrumbs.

4 Heat the oil in a frying pan over medium heat. Fry the chevin rounds until golden on both sides. Remove from heat and drain on paper towel.

5 Arrange the rocket, salad leaves, beetroot and apples on a serving platter. Then, just before serving, place the fried chevin pieces on top of the salad and serve with the dressing.

94

Spicy lamb with artichokes and chickpeas

RECIPE AND STYLING BY **ANKE ROUX** PHOTOGRAPH BY **NEIL CORDER**

Serves 8 **EASY** 60 mins

THE FLAVOUR COMBINATIONS
RUB
30ml olive oil
1 onion, finely sliced
4 bay leaves, chopped
1 large sprig rosemary, chopped
30ml fennel seeds
30ml coriander seeds, crushed
15ml cumin seeds
5ml chilli flakes
5ml ground cinnamon
5ml cloves
salt and freshly ground black
pepper, to taste
30ml brown sugar

1 shoulder of lamb, butterflied
and bone intact
(ask your butcher to do this)
150ml verjuice
1 x 400g tin artichoke
hearts, drained
1 x 410g tin chickpeas, drained
1 bunch mint, chopped

roast potatoes, to serve

HOW TO DO IT

1 Preheat the oven to 220°C. For the rub, heat the olive oil in a pan and fry the onion until soft. Add all of the herbs and spices and fry until the mix is aromatic and the onion starts to caramelise. Remove from the heat, stir in the sugar and allow to cool.

2 Open up the lamb and trim off any excess fat. Lightly pierce the outside fatty skin to allow it to crisp up in the oven.

3 Spread two thirds of the rub over the inside of the lamb. Roll the lamb around the bone so it forms an even roll, and secure with string at regular intervals.

4 Spread the remaining rub over the outside and place the lamb in an oven-to-stovetop roasting tray.

5 Roast for 20 minutes. Reduce the heat to 180°C. Roast for a further 15 minutes per 500g for rare, 20 – 25 minutes per 500g for medium and about 35 minutes or more per 500g for well-done. If the meat has not browned sufficiently at the end of the cooking time, increase the oven heat to the highest setting for the last 15 minutes of cooking.

6 Remove from the oven, place the lamb on a plate and rest for 15 minutes covered in foil.

7 Meanwhile, place the roasting tray over medium heat on the stove and add the verjuice to deglaze the pan. When the pan is sufficiently deglazed, add the artichokes and chickpeas, and heat through. Just before serving, fold through the chopped mint. Adjust the seasoning and pour the verjuice mixture over the lamb. Serve with lashings of the artichoke-and-chickpea sauce and roast potatoes.

97

Olive-and-tomato lasagne

RECIPE AND STYLING BY **NICOLA BASSON** PHOTOGRAPH BY **NEVILLE LOCKHART**

Serves 6 **EASY** 15 mins

THE FLAVOUR COMBINATIONS
12 good-quality egg lasagne sheets
400g cherry tomatoes on the vine
15ml (1 tbsp) olive oil + extra,
to drizzle
salt and freshly ground black
pepper, to taste
120g fresh basil pesto + extra,
to serve
10ml (2 tsp) fresh lemon juice
18 green olives, pitted
12 slices Parma ham
handful fresh basil leaves
150g (about 12) bocconcini

HOW TO DO IT
1 Preheat the oven grill to its highest setting. Place the lasagne sheets in a large saucepan of salted, boiling water. Cook until al dente, about 5–8 minutes. Drain.

2 Place the tomatoes on a baking tray, drizzle with a little olive oil and season. Grill until the tomatoes begin to burst, about 3 minutes.

3 Place the pesto, the 15ml (1 tbsp) olive oil and the lemon juice in a large bowl and season. Add the lasagne sheets and olives, and toss to coat.

4 Layer the lasagne sheets, Parma ham, olives and tomatoes in a serving dish. Top with the basil leaves and bocconcini, drizzle with pesto and serve.

COOK'S TIPS
Bocconcini are bite-sized mozzarella balls. To give this dish an autumnal flavour, replace the tomatoes with roasted butternut and the basil with fresh sage leaves.

Serve on toast
TO SOAK UP
THE YUMMY SAUCE

Spanish calamari

RECIPE BY **KEVIN JOSEPH** PHOTOGRAPH BY **CLINTON FRIEDMAN**

Serves 2 EASY 30 mins

THE FLAVOUR COMBINATIONS
CHILLI BUTTER
50g butter, softened
2 red chillies, seeded
and finely chopped
8 sprigs fresh coriander, chopped
20g red onion, finely chopped
10g garlic paste

PINEAPPLE-AND-PRUNE SALSA
½ fresh pineapple, cubed
5 sprigs fresh coriander,
finely chopped
5 prunes, seeded and chopped
5ml (1 tsp) black sesame seeds
5ml (1 tsp) white sesame seeds
45ml (3 tbsp) tarragon vinegar

SPANISH CALAMARI
15ml (1 tbsp) olive oil
20g chorizo, cut into julienne strips
100g Falkland Island calamari
toasted bread, to serve

HOW TO DO IT

1 For the chilli butter, mix all of the
ingredients together and refrigerate.

2 For the pineapple-and-prune salsa,
mix all of the ingredients together
and set aside.

3 For the Spanish calamari, heat
a frying pan until smoking hot,
add the olive oil and fry the chorizo
for 1 minute. Add the calamari and
chilli butter. Remove from heat.

4 Serve warm on toasted bread with
the pineapple-and-prune salsa.

high

101

Spinach, ham and Parmesan soufflé

RECIPE AND STYLING BY **LYN WOODWARD** PHOTOGRAPH BY **GRAEME WYLLIE**

Serves 6 **EASY** 30 mins

THE FLAVOUR COMBINATIONS

55g butter
**50g Parmesan, finely grated + extra,
to serve**
250g spinach, large stalks removed
30ml (2 tbsp) cake flour
150ml milk, hot
60ml (¼ cup) Cheddar, grated
60ml (¼ cup) ham, finely diced
pinch of ground cayenne pepper
**salt and freshly ground black
pepper, to taste**
2 large eggs, separated

HOW TO DO IT

1. Preheat the oven to 200°C. Grease six 150ml ovenproof ramekins with half of the butter. Scatter half of the Parmesan in the ramekins, swirl to coat and shake off the excess.

2. Bring a pan of water to a boil and cook the spinach for 2 minutes. Drain well, squeeze out the excess water and pat dry with a cloth. Finely chop the spinach and set aside.

3. Melt the remaining butter in a saucepan and stir in the flour to make a roux. Cook for 1 minute, before gradually adding the hot milk. Stir constantly for 2 – 3 minutes. Stir in the Cheddar and remaining Parmesan and remove from the heat. Stir in the spinach, ham and cayenne pepper. Season and stir in the egg yolks.

4. Place the egg whites in a large, spotlessly clean mixing bowl and whisk until stiff peaks form. Using a metal spoon, carefully fold the egg whites into the spinach mixture. Spoon the mixture into the ramekins and place in a roasting dish filled halfway with hot water. Bake for 10 – 12 minutes. Sprinkle with the extra Parmesan and serve.

Exotic mushroom tart with crème fraîche and wild rocket

RECIPE BY **ROZANNE PRESTON** PHOTOGRAPH BY **BRUCE TUCK**

Serves 4 **EASY** 30 mins

THE FLAVOUR COMBINATIONS
400g roll puff pastry, defrosted
2 red onions, sliced
15ml (1 tbsp) olive oil
10ml (2 tsp) balsamic vinegar
5ml (1 tsp) brown sugar
750g exotic mushrooms
fresh thyme, chopped
1 garlic clove, crushed
Parmesan, grated
salt and freshly ground black
pepper, to taste
wild rocket, to serve
crème fraîche, to serve

HOW TO DO IT

1 Preheat the oven to 190°C and heat a baking tray for a few minutes.

2 Fold out the pastry onto a flat baking sheet. Score a border around the pastry with a sharp knife and refrigerate until cool and firm.

3 Place the onions on the baking tray and drizzle with the oil and vinegar. Leave to caramelise for 10 minutes. Sprinkle with the brown sugar and set aside.

4 Fry the mushrooms in a non-stick pan over medium heat until soft and lightly browned, then add the thyme and garlic and stir to combine. Leave to cool slightly.

5 Spread the onion-and-mushroom mixture over the pastry inside the border. Sprinkle with Parmesan and season. Bake until risen and golden, about 20 – 30 minutes.

6 Serve warm with the wild rocket and crème fraîche.

Hot cross bread-and-butter chocolate puddings

RECIPE AND STYLING BY **LEILA SAFFARIAN** ASSISTED BY **NOMVUSELELO MNCUBE** PHOTOGRAPH BY **DYLAN SWART**

Serves 4 **EASY** 40 mins

THE FLAVOUR COMBINATIONS

6 hot cross buns
3 large eggs
125ml (½ cup) fresh cream
125ml (½ cup) milk
2,5ml (½ tsp) ground cinnamon
2,5ml (½ tsp) ground ginger
30ml (2 tbsp) brown sugar
50g raisins
30g (3 tbsp) unsalted butter, softened
50g dark chocolate, cut into chunks
50g white chocolate, cut into chunks
icing sugar, to dust
cocoa powder, to dust

HOW TO DO IT

1 Preheat the oven to 180°C. Slice the tops off the hot cross buns and cut the bottoms into chunks.

2 Combine the eggs, cream, milk, spices and sugar in a medium bowl. Whisk well and add the raisins.

3 Grease four small ovenproof ramekins with butter. Divide the chopped hot cross buns among the pudding bowls.

4 Divide the custard among the bowls and add a few chocolate chunks to each dish. Top with the hot cross bun tops.

5 Bake in the preheated oven until bubbling and the custard is set, about 20 minutes. Remove from oven and serve warm, dusted with icing sugar and cocoa powder.

Pineapple, dark chocolate and granadilla Pavlova

RECIPE AND STYLING BY **ILLANIQUE VAN ASWEGEN** PHOTOGRAPH BY **ADEL FERREIRA** ASSISTED BY **JÖMERI MOUTON**

Serves 4 EASY 2 hrs

THE FLAVOUR COMBINATIONS
60g dark chocolate
3 egg whites
170g castor sugar
10ml (2 tsp) cornflour
10ml (2 tsp) red wine vinegar

FILLING
125ml (½ cup) fresh cream
45ml (3 tbsp) castor sugar
125ml (½ cup) Greek yoghurt
seeds from ½ vanilla pod
½ pineapple, diced
2 granadillas
chocolate shards, to garnish
fresh mint, to garnish

HOW TO DO IT

1 Preheat the oven to 160°C. Line a large, shallow baking tray with baking paper.

2 Melt the chocolate over a double boiler. Allow to cool while you make the meringue.

3 For the meringue, beat the egg whites with an electric whisk until soft peaks form. Add the castor sugar in three batches while continuously whisking, ensuring that the sugar is properly incorporated. Whisk until stiff peaks form and the mixture becomes smooth and glossy.

4 Combine the cornflour and vinegar and whisk into the egg-and-sugar mixture for 20 seconds.

5 Fold in the melted chocolate and spoon the meringue onto the lined tray, moulding it gently into a nest-like shape, slightly smaller than the size of a standard dinner plate. Bake for 40 minutes, turn the oven off and allow to cool down in the oven, about 1 hour.

6 For the filling, use an electric whisk to whip the cream until soft peaks form. Add the sugar in three batches while continuously whisking until stiff. Lightly whisk in the yoghurt and vanilla seeds until smooth.

7 Spoon the mixture onto the cooled meringue and scatter the diced pineapple on top. Add the pulp and seeds from the granadilla, garnish with chocolate shavings and fresh mint, and serve immediately.

109

Pistachio baklava cigars with ginger-and-lemongrass syrup

RECIPE BY **ANNA MONTALI** PHOTOGRAPH BY **GRAEME BORCHERS**

Makes 20 **EASY** 30 mins

THE FLAVOUR COMBINATIONS
150g pistachios, chopped
200g flaked almonds, toasted
20ml (4 tsp) ground cinnamon
10ml (2 tsp) ground cloves
10ml (2 tsp) brown sugar
250g filo pastry
20g butter, melted

GINGER-AND-LEMONGRASS SYRUP
500ml (2 cups) water
250g castor sugar
20ml (4 tsp) lemongrass, sliced
20ml (4 tsp) ginger, chopped

50ml sesame seeds, to serve

HOW TO DO IT

1 Preheat the oven to 180°C. Mix together the pistachios, almonds, cinnamon, cloves and brown sugar and set aside until needed.

2 Lay a sheet of filo pastry on a working surface and cut in half. Brush one half with the melted butter and top with the other half. Sprinkle the nut mixture over the pastry and roll to form a cigar. Lay on a baking tray and brush with butter. Continue with the remaining filo pastry and bake in the oven until golden, about 5 minutes.

3 For the syrup, combine all of the ingredients, except the sesame seeds, in a pot and slowly bring to a boil. Stir until the mixture is syrupy.

4 Remove the cigars from the oven and place on a serving dish. Pour the syrup over, sprinkle with the sesame seeds and serve.

The perfect way
TO ROUND OFF
A MEAL

THE MONTH OF *May*

AS WE APPROACH DARKER, COLDER DAYS,
MAY'S GORGEOUS SELECTION OF DRINKS
AND DISHES IS TASTY, IN SEASON AND
SURE TO WARM THE COCKLES

This recipe was inspired by and adapted from talented foodie, Julie Lindhiem.

Rosemary-scented ginger ale

RECIPE AND STYLING BY **TARYNE JAKOBI** PHOTOGRAPH BY **VANESSA LEWIS**

Makes 1L **EASY** 40 mins +
overnight, to steep

THE FLAVOUR COMBINATIONS
250g fresh ginger, skin on,
coarsely grated
480g brown sugar
peel of 1 lemon
4 sprigs fresh rosemary + extra,
to garnish
300ml lemon juice
500ml (2 cups) water
lemonade, to serve

HOW TO DO IT

1 Place the ginger, 180g of the brown sugar, lemon peel and 2 sprigs of rosemary in a bowl. Bash with the end of a rolling pin to extract the juices. Add the lemon juice and leave to stand, covered, overnight.

2 Whizz the ginger mixture in a food processor and transfer to a heavy-bottomed saucepan. Add the water, 300g brown sugar and remaining rosemary sprigs. Simmer until the liquid has reduced and the mixture forms a syrup, about 30 minutes.

3 Strain the syrup and pour into a sterilised, airtight bottle to cool. Store in the fridge for up to 1 month.

4 To serve, mix the syrup with lemonade and garnish with fresh rosemary sprigs.

French onion soup

RECIPE BY **ANNA MONTALI** ASSISTED BY **NOMVUSELELO MNCUBE** STYLING BY **INGRID CASSON** PHOTOGRAPH BY **KARL ROGERS**

Serves 6 **EASY** 90 mins

THE FLAVOUR COMBINATIONS
70g butter
6 onions, thinly sliced
3 garlic cloves, chopped
2 fresh bay leaves
2 fresh thyme sprigs
500ml (2 cups) water
250ml (1 cup) dry sherry
45ml (3 tbsp) cake flour
1,5L good-quality chicken stock
salt and freshly ground black
pepper, to taste
1 baguette, sliced
200g Gruyère, very thinly sliced

HOW TO DO IT

1 Melt the butter in a large pot over low heat. Add the onions, garlic, bay leaves and thyme. Cook over low heat, stirring occasionally, until the onions are soft and caramelised, about 30 minutes.

2 Add the water and scrape any bits off the bottom of the pot. Simmer until the water has evaporated, about 20 minutes.

3 Stir in the sherry and continue cooking, stirring frequently, until the sherry has evaporated and the onions are dry, about 20 minutes.

4 Discard the bay leaves and thyme and stir in the flour. Add the stock and season. Continue cooking for a further 30 minutes.

5 Preheat the oven grill to high. Place the baguette slices on a baking tray and top with the Gruyère. Grill until the cheese is bubbly and golden, about 5 minutes.

6 Serve the soup hot, topped with the Gruyère croutons.

The creamy texture of the Gorgonzola is offset by the crunchy, toasted walnuts. Served with a toasted baguette, this is real comfort food.

Creamy broccoli-and-Gorgonzola soup with toasted walnuts

RECIPE AND STYLING BY **ALEX BISHOP** PHOTOGRAPH BY **SHANE POWELL**

Serves 6 **EASY** 45 mins

THE FLAVOUR COMBINATIONS
1 large onion, chopped
15ml butter
15ml olive oil
1 head of broccoli,
broken into florets
500ml good-quality chicken stock
100g Gorgonzola, crumbled + extra,
to garnish
60ml fresh cream
salt and freshly ground black
pepper, to taste
walnuts, toasted and crushed,
to garnish

HOW TO DO IT

1 In a large pot, sauté the onion in the butter and olive oil over medium heat until soft and translucent.

2 Add the broccoli florets and stir for 1 minute. Add the chicken stock to just cover the broccoli and simmer for 20 minutes.

3 Transfer to a food processor and blend until smooth. Add the Gorgonzola and cream, stirring to combine. Season to taste.

4 Return to the pot and warm through, but do not allow it to boil.

5 Garnish with toasted walnuts and a couple of chunky pieces of Gorgonzola, and serve.

Roasted parsnips with goat's cheese and winter greens

RECIPE AND STYLING BY **ANKE ROUX** PHOTOGRAPH BY **HENRIQUE WILDING**

Serves 4 – 6 **EASY** 20 mins

THE FLAVOUR COMBINATIONS
400g parsnips, peeled
and halved lengthways
1 garlic bulb, separated into cloves
20ml good-quality olive oil
salt and freshly ground black
pepper, to taste
150g winter greens, like radicchio
and chicory
1 round goat's cheese,
at room temperature
and sliced into wedges
50g hazelnuts, toasted

DRESSING
20ml good-quality olive oil
10ml balsamic vinegar
salt and freshly ground black
pepper, to taste

HOW TO DO IT

1 Preheat the oven to 230°C. Blanch the parsnips in boiling water until almost tender, about 5 minutes. Drain.

2 Toss the blanched parsnips and garlic cloves in the 20ml olive oil and season. Roast in the oven until the parsnips are golden, crispy and slightly charred at the edges, and the garlic cloves are oozy and soft.

3 Arrange the winter greens on a platter and top with the parsnips, garlic cloves, slices of goat's cheese and a scattering of hazelnuts.

4 Mix all of the dressing ingredients together, drizzle over the parsnips and serve warm.

COOK'S TIP
Any winter greens may be used.

Great for lunch
ON A CHILLY
AFTERNOON

Pair this sweet
SIDE DISH WITH
A BEEFY
AND HEARTY MAIN

Roasted pumpkin with salted caramel

RECIPE AND STYLING BY **LEILA SAFFARIAN** ASSISTED BY **NOMVUSELELO MNCUBE** PHOTOGRAPH BY **KARL ROGERS**

Serves 4 **EASY** 35 mins

THE FLAVOUR COMBINATIONS
500g pumpkin, peeled and cubed
30ml (2 tbsp) olive oil
2,5ml (½ tsp) ground coriander
2,5ml (½ tsp) ground cumin
sea salt and freshly ground black
pepper, to taste

CARAMEL
60ml (¼ cup) dark brown sugar
125ml (½ cup) water
5ml (1 tsp) Maldon Sea Salt
microherbs, to serve

HOW TO DO IT

1 Preheat the oven to 200°C. Place the pumpkin in a roasting dish and drizzle with oil. Add the coriander, cumin and seasoning. Mix well and roast until golden, 20 – 25 minutes. Remove from oven and set aside.

2 For the caramel, place the sugar and water in a small saucepan over medium heat and slowly bring to a boil. Cook until a caramel forms, 3 – 4 minutes.

3 Remove from heat and add the Maldon Sea Salt before drizzling over the roasted pumpkin. Serve with microherbs.

Grapefruit, honey and chilli-roasted chicken

RECIPE AND STYLING BY **ILLANIQUE VAN ASWEGEN** PHOTOGRAPH BY **ADEL FERREIRA**

Serves 4 **EASY** 60 mins +
extra, to marinate

THE FLAVOUR COMBINATIONS
250ml (1 cup) grapefruit juice
60ml (¼ cup) sunflower oil
60ml (¼ cup) honey
5ml (1 tsp) chilli flakes
1 garlic clove, crushed
5 sprigs fresh thyme
salt and freshly ground
black pepper, to taste
8 drum and thigh chicken pieces
12 baby onions, peeled
2 grapefruits, sliced into rounds
2 oranges, sliced into rounds
rice or couscous, cooked, to serve
green salad, to serve

HOW TO DO IT

1 Whisk the juice, oil, honey, chilli, garlic and thyme together, transfer to a large sealable plastic bag and season. Place the chicken pieces, along with the peeled onions, in the bag with the marinade and marinate for at least 2 hours or overnight.

2 Preheat the oven to 200°C. Remove the chicken pieces, thyme and onions with a slotted spoon and place in a baking dish. Pour one third of a cup of the marinade over the chicken and roast for 30 – 40 minutes or until golden and tender.

3 Baste the chicken with the pan juices as it cooks. When the chicken has roasted for 20 minutes, add the sliced grapefruits and oranges to the baking dish and roast for another 10 – 15 minutes.

4 Serve with savoury rice or couscous and a green salad.

Great flavours to
SPICE UP YOUR USUAL
ROASTED
CHICKEN

Bouillabaisse

RECIPE AND STYLING BY **LEILA SAFFARIAN** PHOTOGRAPH BY **GRAEME WYLLIE**

Serves 4 **EASY** 45 mins

THE FLAVOUR COMBINATIONS
pinch of saffron threads
15ml (1 tbsp) hot water
3L fish stock
2 x 410g tins chopped tomatoes
1 leek, washed and thinly sliced
1 carrot, peeled and diced
1 celery stick, diced
300g firm white sustainable
fish fillets
15 prawns, cleaned
20 black mussels, scrubbed
and de-bearded
salt and freshly ground
black pepper, to taste
60ml (¼ cup) fresh flat-leaf parsley
leaves, roughly chopped
crusty French bread, to serve

HOW TO DO IT

1 Combine the saffron and hot water in a small bowl and set aside to infuse. Place the fish stock, tomatoes, leek, carrot and celery in a large saucepan and bring to a boil over high heat. Reduce the heat to medium and simmer, uncovered, for 25 minutes.

2 Add the saffron (along with the water in which it has infused) to the tomato mixture, bring to a boil, then reduce the heat to a simmer. Cook for a further 15 minutes until some of the liquid has reduced slightly.

3 Add the fish, prawns and mussels to the soup and cook, covered, for 5 minutes or until the seafood is cooked and the mussels have opened. (Make sure you discard any mussels that remain closed.)

4 Season well and ladle into bowls. Scatter with the parsley and serve with plenty of crusty French bread.

Butternut gnocchi with pan-fried duck breast and mint salsa verde

RECIPE, STYLING AND PHOTOGRAPH BY **KATELYN WILLIAMS**

Serves 4 **EASY** 105 mins

THE FLAVOUR COMBINATIONS
600g starchy potatoes,
whole and skin on
200g whole butternut, skin on
100g cake flour
pinch of ground nutmeg
sea salt and freshly ground
black pepper, to taste
2 egg yolks
4 duck breasts, skin on
and fat scored

SALSA VERDE
handful fresh mint, stalks removed
handful fresh flat-leaf parsley,
stalks removed
1 garlic clove, peeled
30ml (2 tbsp) extra-virgin olive oil
microherbs, to serve

HOW TO DO IT

1 Preheat the oven to 180°C. Place the potatoes and butternut on a baking tray and bake until soft, about 1 hour. Allow to cool slightly, then slice, scoop out the flesh and mash until smooth.

2 Add the flour, nutmeg and seasoning. Mix well.

3 Add the egg yolks and stir until the mixture comes together and leaves the sides of the bowl. Turn out onto a lightly floured work surface and knead until a soft dough forms, about 1 minute.

4 Divide the dough into four and, working with one piece at a time, roll into a long sausage. Cut the gnocchi into 2cm pieces and place on a floured tray.

5 Cook the gnocchi in batches in a large pot of boiling salted water until the gnocchi float to the surface, 3 – 4 minutes. Remove immediately and keep warm.

6 Season the duck breasts well and place skin-side down in a cold pan on medium heat. Cook for 6 – 8 minutes, turn and cook for a further 5 minutes. Set the duck breasts aside to rest for 5 minutes.

7 Add the gnocchi to the duck fat in the pan and sauté until golden.

8 To make the salsa verde, blitz the ingredients in a food processor or blender until combined but not completely smooth.

9 Slice the duck breasts and serve topped with salsa verde and the gnocchi alongside, sprinkled with microherbs.

*These little pies are incredibly moreish and offer
a great new take on the classic Greek spanakopita.*

Baby spinach, feta and piquanté pepper pies

RECIPE AND STYLING BY **LEILA SAFFARIAN** ASSISTED BY **NOMVUSELELO MNCUBE** PHOTOGRAPH BY **ROELENE PRINSLOO**

Makes 12 **EASY** 40 mins

THE FLAVOUR COMBINATIONS
30ml (2 tbsp) olive oil
1 small onion, thinly sliced
200g baby spinach
100g piquanté peppers, chopped
sea salt and freshly ground black
pepper, to taste
small handful fresh coriander,
roughly chopped
150g feta, crumbled
10 sheets filo pastry
100g butter, melted
100g sesame seeds, toasted
fresh coriander leaves, to serve

HOW TO DO IT

1 Preheat the oven to 180°C. Heat the oil in a non-stick frying pan over medium heat. Add the onion and fry until golden.

2 Add the spinach and peppers. Season well and fry for 3 minutes.

3 Remove from heat and add the coriander and feta.

4 Lay two sheets of filo pastry together and cut into four squares of 20cm. Brush with butter and fill each square with 30 – 45ml (2 – 3 tbsp) of the spinach filling.

5 Fold into triangles or roll into cigar shapes. Brush with butter, place on a greased baking tray and scatter with the toasted sesame seeds.

6 Bake in the oven until golden, 8 – 10 minutes. Serve with fresh coriander.

vegetarian

COOK'S TIP
Add cooked, crisp beef mince to the mixture for a meatier version.

Pears poached in cranberry juice with lemon-flavoured mascarpone

RECIPE AND STYLING BY **KAREN SHORT** PHOTOGRAPH BY **GRAEME BORCHERS**

Serves 4 **EASY** 1 hr

THE FLAVOUR COMBINATIONS
750ml (3 cups) cranberry juice
160ml sweet red wine
2 cardamom pods, bruised
60ml (¼ cup) honey
½ vanilla bean, halved lengthways
4 medium pears, peeled

MASCARPONE
250g mascarpone
zest of 2 lemons
juice of 1 lemon
60ml (¼ cup) honey

HOW TO DO IT

1 Combine the cranberry juice, wine, cardamom, 60ml (¼ cup) honey and vanilla bean in a large saucepan. Add the pears and bring to a boil. Reduce the heat, cover and simmer until tender, about 25 minutes. Allow the pears to cool in the syrup. Remove the pears and strain the syrup into a medium heatproof bowl.

2 Return 500ml (2 cups) of the syrup to the same pot; discard any remaining syrup. Bring to a boil, uncovered, until reduced by half, about 15 minutes.

3 For the mascarpone, combine all of the ingredients.

4 Serve the pears hot or cold with the syrup and mascarpone.

COOK'S TIP
The pears can be poached a day ahead.

132

PEARS MAKE A *wonderful dessert* IN WINTER

Apple-rose tartlets

RECIPE AND STYLING BY **SARAH DALL** ASSISTED BY **CLAIRE FERRANDI** PHOTOGRAPH BY **DAWIE VERWEY**

Makes 6 **EASY** 30 mins +
extra, to refrigerate

THE FLAVOUR COMBINATIONS
125g shortcrust pastry, defrosted
icing sugar, to dust

LEMON-MOUSSE FILLING
250ml (1 cup) double-thick cream
20ml (4 tsp) fresh lemon juice
20ml (4 tsp) lemon zest
50g castor sugar

APPLE-ROSE PETALS
2 Granny Smith apples,
peeled and cored
125ml (½ cup) rose water
few drops pale pink
gel food colouring

icing sugar, to serve

HOW TO DO IT

1 Preheat the oven to 200°C.
Roll out the pastry and cut out six 8cm rounds. Line six 6cm-round tart tins with pastry. Cover the pastry with baking paper and fill with baking beans. Blind-bake until the pastry is lightly golden and cooked through, about 10 minutes.

2 For the lemon-mousse filling, combine the cream, lemon juice, lemon zest and castor sugar, and refrigerate until set.

3 For the apple-rose petals, cut the apples into quarters and thinly slice the quarters. Place the apple slices, rose water and colouring in a small pot and simmer until the apple is soft, about 2 minutes. Remove from heat and set aside to cool.

4 To assemble the tarts, spoon the lemon filling into the tart cases. To make the apple roses, twirl a piece of poached apple to resemble a rose bud and place in the centre of the tart. Layer pieces of poached apple around the central bud in the formation of petals until the apple pieces resemble a rose. Repeat for all tarts and place in the fridge for 30 minutes.

5 Dust lightly with icing sugar just before serving.

135

Macaroons with white-chocolate ganache

RECIPE AND STYLING BY **TONI SCORGIE** AND **NADINE WANER** PHOTOGRAPH BY **GRAEME BORCHERS**

Makes 30 **EASY** 60 mins

THE FLAVOUR COMBINATIONS
MACAROONS
200g icing sugar
60ml (¼ cup) cocoa powder
120g ground almonds
3 large egg whites
30ml (2 tbsp) castor sugar

GANACHE
50ml fresh cream
110g white chocolate, diced
50g icing sugar
edible gold leaf, to serve

HOW TO DO IT

1 Preheat the oven to 160°C. To make the macaroons, sift the icing sugar, cocoa and almonds into a bowl and mix well.

2 In a separate bowl, beat the egg whites and sugar until stiff. Fold in the dry ingredients until combined.

3 Place spoonfuls of the mixture on a lined baking tray and leave to stand for 10 minutes.

4 Bake until crispy on the outside, 10 – 15 minutes. Remove from oven and leave to cool.

5 For the ganache, heat the cream in a saucepan until almost boiling. Stir in the chocolate until melted. Add the icing sugar and mix until smooth. Allow to cool slightly.

6 Sandwich the macaroons together with the ganache and serve with the gold leaf sprinkled over.

THE MONTH OF *June*

WE CAN'T WAIT FOR YOU TO DROOL YOUR WAY THROUGH JUNE'S
MOREISH MEDLEY OF INDULGENT DISHES, PERFECT FOR NIGHTS
IN, COSIED UP BY THE FIRE WITH A GLASS (OR THREE) OF RED.
THE COQ AU VIN IS DEFINITELY ONE TO CHERISH THIS WINTER…

*Also known as bullshots,
these are fabulous winter warmers.
Serve them as your guests arrive.*

Consommé with chilli sherry

RECIPE AND STYLING BY **VICKI CLARKE** AND **NIKKI WEFELMEIER** PHOTOGRAPH BY **GRAEME BORCHERS**

Makes 12 **EASY** 10 mins + 2 days, to infuse

THE FLAVOUR COMBINATIONS
6 hot chillies
750ml bottle sherry
1L (4 cups) good-quality chicken/ beef stock
30ml (2 tbsp) soya sauce

fresh spring onions, sliced, to garnish

HOW TO DO IT

1 A few days before making this dish, place the chillies in the bottle of sherry and leave them to infuse.

2 For the consommé, heat the stock, add the soya sauce and bring to a rolling boil. Stir in about 60ml (¼ cup) of the chilli sherry and pour the soup into espresso cups.

3 Top with a few spring onions and serve hot.

COOK'S TIP
Chilli sherry is very handy – it keeps for ages and is wonderful for adding to soups or even a mushroom sauce.

Sweet potato soup with maple-and-whisky glazed bacon

RECIPE AND STYLING BY **JACQUES ERASMUS** PHOTOGRAPH BY **MYBURGH DU PLESSIS**

Serves 6 **EASY** 45 mins

THE FLAVOUR COMBINATIONS
450g sweet potatoes, peeled and
roughly chopped
250ml (1 cup) orange juice
175g butter
5ml (1 tsp) orange zest
salt and freshly ground black
pepper, to taste
250g streaky bacon
45ml (3 tbsp) maple syrup
45ml (3 tbsp) whisky
25ml fresh chives, finely chopped,
to garnish

HOW TO DO IT

1 Preheat the oven to 180°C. Place the sweet potatoes in a saucepan and add the orange juice and some water to just cover. Bring to a boil and cook until the potatoes are soft, 20 minutes. Allow to cool a little before transferring the potatoes and liquid to a liquidiser, along with the butter and orange zest. Blend until smooth, adding a little more water to make a thick soup. Season to taste.

2 Lay out the bacon on a baking tray and place a second tray on top, so that it presses the bacon flat. Cook in the oven, 10 minutes, then remove and take off the top baking tray.

3 Combine the maple syrup and whisky and pour the mixture over the bacon. Return to the oven and bake until golden and sticky, 2 – 3 minutes.

4 Spoon the soup into a tureen or individual serving bowls. Top with the bacon, drizzle with the pan juices and garnish with fresh chives.

142

Roasted winter squash with pumpkin seeds and thyme

RECIPE AND STYLING BY **VICKI CLARKE** AND **NIKKI WEFELMEIER** PHOTOGRAPH BY **ELSA YOUNG**

Serves 4 **EASY** 40 mins

THE FLAVOUR COMBINATIONS
1kg mixed squash, peeled,
seeded and diced
(we used butternut,
hubbard and pumpkin)
100g raw pumpkin seeds
50ml olive oil
Maldon Sea Salt and freshly ground
black pepper, to taste
60g fresh thyme, roughly chopped
500g mixed baby gem squash
and pattypans

HOW TO DO IT

1 Preheat the oven to 200°C. Place the squash, pumpkin seeds and olive oil in a roasting pan and season.

2 Add the thyme and roast, tossing once, about 20 minutes.

3 Remove from oven, toss again and add the baby gem squash and pattypans.

4 Roast until soft and golden, about 15 minutes.

5 Serve immediately or reheat when ready.

*This dish is the perfect accompaniment to
roast chicken and mash on a cold night.*

Potato, garlic and thyme tortilla with caramelised fennel

RECIPE AND STYLING BY **THULISA MARTINS** PHOTOGRAPH BY **DYLAN SWART**

Serves 4 **EASY** 80 mins

THE FLAVOUR COMBINATIONS
TORTILLA
1 onion, chopped
4 sprigs fresh thyme leaves
2 garlic cloves, crushed
90ml olive oil
6 floury potatoes, peeled
and thinly sliced with
a vegetable peeler
Maldon Sea Salt and freshly ground
black pepper, to taste
6 large eggs, beaten

CARAMELISED FENNEL
125ml (½ cup) malt vinegar
45g brown sugar
500g baby fennel, trimmed
and halved lengthways
Maldon Sea Salt and freshly ground
black pepper, to taste
½ red pepper, chopped, to serve

HOW TO DO IT

1 Heat a large saucepan over medium-high heat and sauté the onion, thyme leaves and garlic in 80ml of the olive oil until the onion is soft and translucent, about 15 minutes. Reduce the heat to low, add the potatoes and fry, while stirring, until cooked, 15 – 30 minutes. Season while the mixture is still warm and add the eggs. Stir until everything is well combined.

2 Heat a separate non-stick frying pan, big enough to perfectly fit the mixture, over low heat and add the remaining 10ml olive oil. Add the potato mixture and fry while stirring, about 1 minute. Smooth the mixture by pressing it down with a wooden spoon to form the shape of the pan and fry until firm, about 10 minutes. Turn the tortilla out by clamping a flat lid or a plate on top and turning the pan upside down. Return the pan to the heat and slide the tortilla back in to brown the reverse side, about 5 minutes. Allow to cool completely in the pan.

3 For the caramelised fennel, heat the vinegar and sugar together in a separate frying pan over medium heat. Add the fennel and season. Cook until the fennel is caramelised and syrupy, about 10 minutes. Serve with the tortilla while both are still warm, sprinkled with red pepper.

COOK'S TIP
If the fennel becomes too crystallised while caramelising, stir in the juice of 1 lemon.

Five-spice hoisin ribs

RECIPE AND STYLING BY **VICKI CLARKE** AND **NIKKI WEFELMEIER** PHOTOGRAPH BY **GRAEME BORCHERS**

Makes 30 **EASY** 30 mins

THE FLAVOUR COMBINATIONS
1,5kg pork ribs, cut into singles
and then in half
5ml five-spice powder
salt and freshly ground black
pepper, to taste
5 spring onions, finely sliced
lengthways, to garnish

SAUCE
45ml olive oil
2 garlic cloves, crushed
10ml root ginger, grated
60ml hoisin sauce
30ml sweet-chilli sauce
30ml soya sauce
60ml honey

HOW TO DO IT

1 Preheat the oven to 140°C. Rub the ribs with the five-spice powder and season.

2 Place the ribs in an ovenproof dish, cover with foil and roast for 1 hour.

3 To make the sauce, heat the olive oil and fry the garlic and ginger. Add all of the other ingredients and stir for 1 minute.

4 Remove the ribs from the oven and add them to the sauce. Cover and return to the oven for 30 minutes. Take off the cover and cook for a further 30 minutes.

5 To serve, stack the ribs on dishes and garnish with the spring onion.

COOK'S TIP
To make things easier, you can cook the ribs earlier in the day, refrigerate and warm when you need them. Beef can be substituted for pork.

149

Coq au vin with barley-and-spinach dumplings

RECIPE BY **NEIL ROAKE** STYLING BY **NEIL ROAKE** AND **KELLY CHRYSTAL** PHOTOGRAPH BY **CRAIG SCOTT**

Serves 4 – 6 **EASY** 2 hrs 15 mins

THE FLAVOUR COMBINATIONS
90ml olive oil
250g smoked bacon, diced
2 onions, peeled and finely diced
3 garlic cloves, peeled and sliced
1,5kg free-range whole chicken,
legs trussed with string
salt and freshly ground
black pepper, to taste
750ml (3 cups) red wine
250ml (1 cup) chicken stock
10 fresh thyme sprigs + extra,
to garnish
500g pearl onions, peeled
500g button mushrooms
8 – 12 baby carrots
20 strips pancetta, fried until crisp,
to serve (optional)

DUMPLINGS
200g pearl barley, rinsed well
750ml (3 cups) water
200g baby-leaf spinach, rinsed
1 small onion, peeled and chopped
1 garlic clove, peeled and
finely chopped
45ml (3 tbsp) fresh parsley, chopped
2 eggs
40g Parmesan, grated
2,5ml (½ tsp) salt
1,25ml (¼ tsp) ground black pepper
75g cake flour
1L (4 cups) vegetable broth,
to poach

HOW TO DO IT

1 Preheat the oven to 180°C. Heat 30ml (2 tbsp) of the olive oil in a large, heavy-based pan over medium heat. Add the bacon and cook until lightly browned, 5 – 8 minutes. Add the onions and garlic and continue to cook until the onions are translucent, 10 minutes. Remove the onion mixture and set aside.

2 Clean out the pan and add another 30ml (2 tbsp) of the olive oil. Liberally sprinkle the chicken with salt and black pepper on both sides. Add the chicken to the pan, breast side down, and cook over medium heat until the skin turns golden, 5 minutes. Turn the chicken over and brown the other side. Return the onion mixture to the pot and add the red wine, stock and thyme. Put the lid on and simmer over medium heat, 30 minutes.

3 Place the pearl onions, cut edge down, in a griddle pan over medium heat and brown the edges. Remove and set aside. Add the mushrooms and final 30ml (2 tbsp) of the olive oil to the griddle pan and cook until the mushrooms just start to brown and soften, about 10 minutes. Place the onions, mushrooms and carrots in the pot with the chicken, ensuring that they remain on top. Put the lid on and place in the oven, 30 minutes.

4 For the dumplings, rinse the barley and place in a pot over medium heat with the water and cook until tender, 45 minutes. Drain in a colander, squeezing out any excess moisture. Set aside to cool.

5 Rinse the spinach in water, drain and add to a saucepan. Over low heat, sauté until just wilted. Remove from heat and set aside to cool. Squeeze out any excess moisture.

6 Add the barley, spinach, onion, garlic, parsley, eggs, cheese, salt, pepper and flour to a food processor and pulse until smooth. Place in a bowl and refrigerate, 15 minutes. Dust your hands with flour and roll the mixture into dumplings about the size of ping-pong balls.

7 Heat the stock over medium heat and gently poach the dumplings, 3 minutes. Remove with a slotted spoon.

8 Five minutes before serving, add the cooked dumplings to the coq au vin so they just heat through. Serve with the crispy pancetta, if desired, and garnish with a sprig of fresh thyme.

COOK'S TIP
If you prefer a thicker broth, simply mash 15g butter with 15ml (1 tbsp) cake flour. Drop small amounts at a time into the broth and whisk.

Fish tacos

RECIPE AND STYLING BY **THOMAS HUGHES** PHOTOGRAPH BY **GRAEME WYLLIE**

Serves 6 **EASY** 1 hr

**THE FLAVOUR COMBINATIONS
MARINADE**
1 jalapeño, seeded and chopped
250ml (1 cup) olive oil
**handful fresh parsley, coriander and
mint, chopped**
30g (½ cup) fresh ginger, grated
**salt and freshly ground black
pepper, to taste**

**180g sustainable fresh white fish
(like hake), skinned, pin-boned and
cut into bite-sized pieces**

TOMATO-AND-CORIANDER SALSA
6 tomatoes, seeded and diced
1 chilli, seeded and chopped
juice of 1 lime
**small handful fresh coriander
leaves, chopped**
¼ red onion, peeled and chopped
1 garlic clove, peeled and crushed
**salt and freshly ground black
pepper, to taste**

BEER-BATTERED FISH
250ml (1 cup) draught beer
125ml (½ cup) soda water
**220g self-raising flour, to thicken
until the mixture slides gently off
the fish**
oil, to deep-fry

TO SERVE
12 taco shells
200g guacamole
115g (½ cup) crème fraîche
small handful shredded lettuce
small handful fresh coriander leaves
2 limes, cut into wedges

HOW TO DO IT

1 For the marinade, mix all of the ingredients together in a large bowl. Add the pieces of fish and cover with cling film. Refrigerate to marinate, 30 minutes.

2 For the salsa, mix all of the ingredients together and set aside.

3 For the beer batter, mix the beer and soda water together in a bowl. Season to taste and whisk in the flour until a ribbon effect is reached.

4 Heat the oil in a deep-fryer or deep pot to 180°C. Dip the marinated fish into the batter and deep-fry until golden brown, about 3 minutes.

5 To assemble the tacos, fill the shells with guacamole, crème fraîche, lettuce and coriander, as desired. Top with pieces of deep-fried fish and serve with the salsa and lime wedges.

153

Editor's choice

Osso buco Milanese

RECIPE AND STYLING BY **LEILA SAFFARIAN** ASSISTED BY **NOMVUSELELO MNCUBE** PHOTOGRAPH BY **GRAEME WYLLIE**

Serves 4 **EASY** 120 mins

THE FLAVOUR COMBINATIONS
30ml (2 tbsp) olive oil
8 beef shins
30ml (2 tbsp) cake flour
20g (2 tbsp) butter
1 onion, chopped
½ celery stick, chopped
salt and freshly ground black
pepper, to taste
125ml (½ cup) dry white wine
375ml (1½ cups) beef stock
fresh crusty bread, to serve

GREMOLATA
zest of 1 lemon, grated
1 garlic clove, chopped
30ml (2 tbsp) fresh flat-leaf
parsley, chopped

HOW TO DO IT

1 Heat the oil in a large non-stick frying pan over medium-high heat.

2 Lightly dust the beef shins with flour and fry in batches until brown. Transfer to a plate and set aside.

3 Add the butter and chopped vegetables to the pan. Season and cook over low heat for 5 – 6 minutes. Return the meat to the pan and add the wine.

4 Add the stock and reduce the heat to low, cover with a tight-fitting lid and cook gently until the meat is tender, about 1½ hours.

5 For the gremolata, combine all of the ingredients.

6 Spoon the osso buco into serving bowls and scatter with the gremolata just before serving. Make sure there is plenty of crusty bread to mop up all the rich gravy.

COOK'S TIP
Beef shin is a delicious substitute for the more traditional veal shin.

Coconut chicken fusion pizza

RECIPE AND STYLING BY **ODETTE WILLIAMS** PHOTOGRAPH SUPPLIED

Makes 1 **EASY** 60 mins + 2 hrs, to prove

THE FLAVOUR COMBINATIONS
PIZZA DOUGH
10g instant dry yeast
30ml (2 tbsp) honey
lukewarm water
500g cake flour
5ml (1 tsp) salt
30ml (2 tbsp) olive oil
semolina, to dust

TOPPING
100ml tomato passata
100g chicken breast, poached and
finely shredded
50ml coconut milk
30ml (2 tbsp) dukkah
35ml soya sauce
50g mozzarella, grated
50g Cheddar, grated
50ml yoghurt
bean sprouts
fresh coriander leaves

HOW TO DO IT

1 For the dough, mix the 10g yeast with the honey and a little lukewarm water.

2 In another bowl, mix the cake flour and salt. Transfer to a clean working surface. Make a well in the centre and pour in the yeast mixture and the olive oil. Using your fingertips in a circular motion, slowly mix in the flour to create a sticky batter. Dust your hands with flour and keep mixing, adding water until the dough starts to cling together and is less sticky. Make sure that all the flour is mixed into the dough. Shape it into a ball and place on a floured surface. Knead until the dough is elastic, about 5 minutes. Dust the top with flour and place in a bowl covered with a damp tea towel. Set aside in a warm place to prove for about 2 hours. Knock the air out by squashing it. Divide the dough into four pieces and set aside.

3 Preheat the oven grill to 200°C. Lightly dust a work surface with semolina and roll one piece of dough very thinly into a 30cm disc. Place on a pizza tray and prick all over with a fork. Bake for 1 minute.

4 For the topping, spread the passata over the base. Mix together the poached and finely shredded chicken breast, coconut milk, dukkah and 15ml (1 tbsp) of the soya sauce.

5 Scatter the chicken mixture evenly over the passata. Sprinkle with the grated mozzarella and Cheddar. Return to the oven and bake until the cheese is melted and the base is crisp, about 5 minutes.

6 Whisk together the yoghurt and 20ml (4 tsp) of the remaining soya sauce and pour into a squeeze bottle.

7 Remove the pizza from the oven and sprinkle with bean sprouts. Drizzle with the yoghurt mixture and scatter over fresh coriander leaves. Serve hot.

COOK'S TIP
The remaining pizza dough can be frozen for up to 3 months.

Spinach pancake cannelloni

RECIPE AND STYLING BY **ANNA MONTALI** PHOTOGRAPH BY **ROELENE PRINSLOO**

Serves 4 **EASY** 50 mins

THE FLAVOUR COMBINATIONS
PANCAKES
250ml (1 cup) milk
90g cake flour
4 large eggs
a pinch of salt

FILLING
300g baby spinach,
cooked and chopped
60g Parmesan, freshly grated +
extra, to sprinkle
250g fresh ricotta
10ml (2 tsp) ground nutmeg
salt and freshly ground
black pepper, to taste
20g (2 tbsp) butter
blue-cheese dressing, to serve

HOW TO DO IT

1 To make the pancakes, mix the milk, flour, one egg and salt until well combined. Cover and leave to rest for 20 minutes.

2 Heat a small non-stick frying pan and pour in enough of the milk mixture to lightly cover the base of the pan. Cook for a few seconds, then turn over and cook the other side. Stack and continue until all of the milk mixture has been used.

3 Preheat the oven to 180°C. For the filling, mix the spinach, Parmesan, ricotta and nutmeg, and season.

4 Place two pancakes diagonally opposite in a loaf tin and set aside. Fill the remaining pancakes with the spinach mixture and roll to form a cigar. Place neatly in the tin and stack.

5 Mix the butter and remaining eggs together and pour over the pancakes. Sprinkle with extra Parmesan and bake for 30 minutes. Remove, slice, drizzle with the dressing and serve.

Upside-down pear cake

RECIPE AND STYLING BY **ANNA MONTALI** ASSISTED BY **NOMVUSELELO MNCUBE** PHOTOGRAPH BY **VANESSA LEWIS**

Makes 1 cake **EASY** 1 hr 50 mins

THE FLAVOUR COMBINATIONS

**100g sugar + extra,
to sprinkle
2 x 400g tins baby pears, drained
1 large egg
1,5L (6 cups) milk
5ml (1 tsp) bicarbonate of soda
120g butter
100ml honey
220g '00' flour
pinch salt**

**castor sugar, to dust
whipped cream, to serve (optional)**

HOW TO DO IT

1 Preheat the oven to 180°C. Lightly butter a 26cm-round springform cake tin and sprinkle all over with a little sugar. Arrange the pears at the bottom of the tin.

2 In a mixing bowl, beat the egg with the milk and bicarbonate of soda and set aside.

3 In a saucepan, melt the butter and honey over low heat and set aside.

4 Sift the flour and salt into a large mixing bowl. Add the egg mixture, the butter mixture and the 100g sugar, and beat well using a hand-held electric mixer.

5 Pour the batter over the pears and bake, about 50 minutes. Leave to cool completely, then refrigerate for about 30 minutes. The cake will be very soft before refrigerating.

6 Serve dusted with castor sugar and with a side of whipped cream, if desired.

Tiramisu cake

RECIPE AND STYLING BY **MARWAN AL SAYED** PHOTOGRAPH BY **GRAEME WYLLIE**

Makes 1 **EASY** 40 mins + 2 hrs, to set

THE FLAVOUR COMBINATIONS
SPONGE
7 large egg whites
280g castor sugar
7 large egg yolks, lightly beaten
110g cornflour
110g cake flour
cocoa powder, to serve
chocolate shavings, to serve
icing sugar, to serve

SYRUP
60ml (¼ cup) instant coffee granules
50ml boiling water
100ml coffee liqueur (optional)
500g mascarpone, at room temperature
4 large eggs
80g castor sugar

HOW TO DO IT

1 Preheat the oven to 200°C. To make the sponge, beat the egg whites to soft peaks. Gradually add the 280g castor sugar while beating until a glossy meringue is formed. Fold in the egg yolks until just combined, making sure you do not overmix. Sift the cornflour and cake flour together and fold into the wet ingredients until just combined.

2 Roll out enough baking paper to fit a baking tray. Mark out two 20cm circles on the baking paper and lightly grease.

3 Spoon the sponge mixture into a piping bag and pipe into the circular outlines using a spiral motion. Repeat until you have four circles. Bake until light brown, about 10 minutes. Allow to cool completely.

4 To make the syrup, mix the instant coffee granules with the boiling water and add the liqueur, if desired. Mix well.

5 In a separate bowl, beat the eggs with the 80g castor sugar until pale and fluffy, about 10 minutes. Fold in the mascarpone and set aside.

6 To assemble the cake, trim the cake layers if necessary and slide one sponge circle into a 20cm-round springform cake tin and brush with enough syrup to soak into the sponge.

7 Use a spatula to apply a 2cm layer of the mascarpone mixture on top of the sponge, then top the mascarpone with another sponge round. Repeat the layering of sponge and mascarpone, ending with a layer of mascarpone. Place in the fridge until set, about 2 hours, or overnight.

8 Serve at room temperature dusted with cocoa powder, chocolate shavings and icing sugar.

THE MONTH OF *July*

FROM PASTA AND PARSNIPS TO CURRIES, STEWS AND IRRESISTIBLE CRUMBLES AND TARTS, WE'VE GOT YOUR JULY SMORGASBORD SORTED. SHARING HEART-WARMING DISHES RICH IN FLAVOUR WILL HAVE FRIENDS AND FAMILY HEADING FOR SECONDS (AND EVEN THIRDS) AND SITTING ROUND THE TABLE UNTIL THE EARLY HOURS…

Avocado mousse topped with cauliflower and bacon crumbs

RECIPE AND STYLING BY **ILLANIQUE VAN ASWEGEN** PHOTOGRAPH BY **ADEL FERREIRA** ASSISTED BY **JÖMERI MOUTON**

Serves 6 **EASY** 40 mins

THE FLAVOUR COMBINATIONS
AVOCADO MOUSSE
3 avocados, peeled
and pitted
juice of 1 small lemon
15ml (1 tbsp) creamed horseradish
5ml (1 tsp) wholegrain mustard
125ml (½ cup) sour cream
salt and freshly ground black pepper,
to taste

CAULIFLOWER AND BACON CRUMBS
250g streaky bacon
150g cauliflower florets, washed
30ml (2 tbsp) fresh chives, chopped

watercress, to garnish (optional)
small cauliflower florets, to garnish
sourdough/Melba toast, to serve

HOW TO DO IT

1 Preheat the oven to grill. For the mousse, blitz everything together in a blender until smooth. Season to taste. Divide the mixture among 6 small serving glasses and refrigerate to set.

2 For the crumbs, place the bacon on a lined baking tray and grill until golden and crisp, 10 – 15 minutes. Place the raw cauliflower in a food processor and blitz until it resembles coarse breadcrumbs. Heat a dry pan over high heat, add the cauliflower crumbs and toast until golden and crisp, 5 – 7 minutes. Keep a close eye on them to prevent burning.

3 Place the crispy bacon in the food processor and blitz until it resembles coarse breadcrumbs. Add to the pan with the cauliflower, stir to combine and cook, 5 minutes. Remove from heat and stir in the chopped chives.

4 Remove the mousse from the fridge, spoon some of the crumbs on top and garnish with watercress, if desired, and cauliflower florets. Serve with the toast on the side.

COOK'S TIPS
This dish is best served as individual starters. Serve the mousse in pretty glasses with long spoons. You can also serve it in a big dish as a spread or dip to which guests can help themselves.

Prawn and angel-hair pasta soup

RECIPE AND STYLING BY **ANNA MONTALI** PHOTOGRAPH BY **GRAEME BORCHERS**

Serves 4 **EASY** 15 mins

THE FLAVOUR COMBINATIONS
20ml (4 tsp) olive oil
10g butter
2 garlic cloves, peeled and
finely chopped
2cm fresh ginger, peeled and grated
1L (4 cups) fish stock
80g string beans, sliced
12 prawns, peeled and deveined,
tails left intact
2 spring onions, sliced
120g angel-hair pasta
salt and freshly ground black
pepper, to taste

coriander leaves, to garnish

HOW TO DO IT
1 Heat the oil and butter in a heavy-based pot over low heat and sauté the garlic and ginger, 2 minutes.
2 Add the stock and bring to a boil. Reduce the heat, add the beans, prawns and spring onion and continue to cook for a further 5 minutes.
3 Add the pasta and season to taste. Cook until al dente, about 5 minutes.
4 Pour the soup into bowls and garnish with coriander before serving.

COOK'S TIP
For a lemony twist, add a few leaves of lemon verbena to the stock.

Editor's choice

Maple-roasted parsnip soup with dukkah-dusted parsnip crisps

RECIPE AND STYLING BY **TARYNE JAKOBI** PHOTOGRAPH BY **VANESSA LEWIS**

Serves 8 **EASY** 1 hr 10 mins

THE FLAVOUR COMBINATIONS
PARSNIP CRISPS
4 large parsnips, peeled
80g butter, melted
50ml brown sugar
50ml dukkah

SOUP
900g parsnips, washed and chopped
50g butter
60ml (¼ cup) olive oil
1 large onion, peeled and chopped
100ml maple syrup
200g potatoes, peeled and cubed
1,5L (6 cups) chicken stock
salt and freshly ground black pepper, to taste

HOW TO DO IT

1 For the parsnip crisps, preheat the oven to 200°C and line a baking tray with baking paper.

2 Using a vegetable peeler, slice the 4 parsnips into thin ribbons. Combine the 80g melted butter, sugar and dukkah in a bowl. Toss the parsnip ribbons into this mixture until well coated, place them on the baking tray and roast, 10 minutes. Toss and return to the oven until crispy and golden, 5 – 10 minutes. Set aside until needed. Leave the oven on.

3 For the soup, toss the 900g parsnips in the 50g butter and the olive oil and roast for 20 minutes. Add the onion, pour over the maple syrup and roast for a further 15 minutes.

4 Transfer the parsnips to a soup pot, add the potatoes and stock and bring to a boil. Season to taste and skim often to remove any scum.

5 Reduce the heat and simmer until the potatoes are tender, about 20 minutes. Allow to cool slightly. Transfer to a food processor and blend until smooth. Serve hot with the parsnip crisps.

171

Warm chickpea curry with roasted vegetables served on bulgur wheat

RECIPE AND STYLING BY **NIKKI GASKELL** AND **ROBYN TIMSON** PHOTOGRAPH BY **GRAEME BORCHERS**

Serves 4 **EASY** 1 hr 10 mins

THE FLAVOUR COMBINATIONS
1L (4 cups) boiling water
500ml (2 cups) bulgur wheat,
uncooked
½ butternut, diced
4 baby turnips, diced
2 small parsnips, diced
10 baby carrots
15ml (1 tbsp) olive oil
2 x 410g tins chickpeas,
drained and rinsed
1 x 410g tin peeled
chopped tomatoes
250ml (1 cup) good-quality
vegetable stock
10ml (2 tsp) dried chilli flakes
15ml (1 tbsp) cumin seeds
15ml (1 tbsp) ground cinnamon
15ml (1 tbsp) ground coriander

fresh coriander, chopped, to garnish
Greek yoghurt, to serve (optional)

HOW TO DO IT

1 Preheat the oven to 200°C. Add the water to the bulgur wheat, cover and leave to stand, 20 minutes.

2 For the curry, place all of the fresh vegetables on a baking tray, drizzle with the oil and bake until the edges are golden, about 15 minutes.

3 Combine the vegetables in a pot along with the chickpeas, tomatoes, stock and dried spices and allow to simmer, about 45 minutes.

4 Serve on a bed of bulgur wheat, garnished with fresh coriander and some thick Greek yoghurt, if desired.

This dish must be simmered slowly and is absolutely delicious mopped up with French baguette. Yum!

Hearty cinnamon beef stew with port, shallots and streaky bacon

RECIPE BY **KAREN SHORT** STYLING BY **COLETTE LE CLUS** AND **LEIGH MILES** PHOTOGRAPH BY **GRAEME BORCHERS**

Serves 6 **EASY** 3 hrs 20 mins

THE FLAVOUR COMBINATIONS
30ml (2 tbsp) olive oil
130g streaky bacon, rind removed, finely chopped
1kg stewing beef, cut into 3cm cubes
60ml (¼ cup) red wine vinegar
16 shallots, peeled and left whole without cutting through the root
20ml (4 tsp) tomato purée
6 garlic cloves, peeled and chopped
10ml (2 tsp) cake flour
2 fresh bay leaves
5ml (1 tsp) fresh thyme, chopped
1 x 5cm piece orange peel, thinly pared
1 cinnamon stick
80g black olives, pitted
250ml (1 cup) port
1L (4 cups) hot beef stock (or enough to cover the meat)
salt and freshly ground black pepper, to taste

fresh flat-leaf parsley, chopped, to serve
parsley rice, to serve (see 'Cook's tips')
French baguettes, to serve

HOW TO DO IT

1 Preheat the oven to 150°C. Heat 15ml (1 tbsp) of the olive oil in an ovenproof pot over medium heat. Add the bacon and cook, 5 minutes. Set aside in a large bowl.

2 Brown the beef in batches in the same pot and add to the bacon.

3 Add the vinegar to the pot and allow to bubble until reduced by half. Pour over the beef and the bacon.

4 Heat the remaining oil in the pot, add the shallots and cook, stirring continuously, until lightly golden, about 5 minutes.

5 Add the tomato purée, garlic and flour and cook for 1 minute before returning the beef, bacon and vinegar to the pot.

6 Add the bay leaves, thyme, orange peel, cinnamon and olives and stir to combine. Pour in the port and bring to a simmer. Add enough stock so that the liquid level is no more than a couple of centimetres below the surface of the meat. Put the lid on the pot and place in the oven to stew gently, 3 hours.

7 Remove the cinnamon stick and bay leaves. Season and add the parsley. Serve with fluffy parsley rice and French baguettes.

COOK'S TIPS
Peel shallots by soaking them in boiling water for 10 minutes. Drain and rinse under cold water, then peel with a knife. For parsley rice, simply add freshly chopped flat-leaf parsley to the cooked rice and toss well.

175

Smoorsnoek with crispy potato röstis, basil pesto, crème fraîche and watercress

RECIPE BY **IAN BERGH** STYLING BY **SHELLY BERGH** PHOTOGRAPH BY **SHANE POWELL**

Serves 4 **EASY** 30 mins

THE FLAVOUR COMBINATIONS
RÖSTIS
2 medium potatoes, peeled
1 large egg, whisked
15ml (1 tbsp) cake flour
salt and freshly ground black
pepper, to taste
15ml (1 tbsp) oil

125ml (½ cup) caramelised onions
400g smoked snoek, shredded and
bones removed
60ml (¼ cup) basil pesto
60ml (¼ cup) crème fraîche, watered
down slightly to form a sauce

spring onions, sliced, to serve
tomato cubes, to serve
80g watercress, washed and dried,
to garnish

HOW TO DO IT

1 For the röstis, grate the potatoes and squeeze out all of the liquid.

2 Add half of the egg, all of the flour and seasoning to the grated potato. Discard the remaining egg.

3 Heat the oil in a frying pan and add 15ml (1 tbsp) grated potato mixture. Flatten this a little with the back of a spoon and fry on each side until golden brown and cooked through, about 4 minutes. Remove from pan and drain on paper towel. Repeat with the remaining mixture. Set the röstis aside and keep warm.

4 Mix the caramelised onion and snoek together.

5 Place the röstis on serving plates. Spoon some snoek mixture over and drizzle with the pesto and crème fraîche. Garnish with sliced spring onions, tomato cubes and watercress and serve immediately.

Spaghetti with beetroot pesto

RECIPE AND STYLING BY **ANKE ROUX** PHOTOGRAPH BY **NEIL CORDER**

Serves 4 **EASY** 2 hrs

THE FLAVOUR COMBINATIONS
250g beetroot, cooked and peeled
50ml olive oil + extra, to serve
handful Parmesan, grated + extra,
to serve
15ml (1 tbsp) pine nuts, toasted
1 chilli, seeded and chopped (optional)
juice and zest of 1 lemon
salt and freshly ground black pepper,
to taste
500g spaghetti

HOW TO DO IT

1 Combine all of the ingredients, except the spaghetti, in a blender and blitz until smooth. Taste and adjust the seasoning, if necessary.

2 Cook the spaghetti in plenty of boiling water until al dente. Drain.

3 Toss the pesto through the hot spaghetti and serve immediately, sprinkled with extra Parmesan and drizzled with olive oil.

Tomato, olive and anchovy tarte Tatin

RECIPE AND STYLING BY **SUE GREIG** PHOTOGRAPH BY **GRAEME BORCHERS**

Makes 6 **EASY** 30 mins

THE FLAVOUR COMBINATIONS
**9 Roma tomatoes, blanched
and peeled
handful Kalamata olives, pitted
180ml red-onion jam
1 x 400g roll puff pastry, defrosted
and cut into six 10cm rounds
large handful rocket leaves
lemon juice, to taste
olive oil, to taste
12 anchovy fillets**

**Parmesan shavings, to serve
balsamic vinegar, to drizzle**

HOW TO DO IT

1 Preheat the oven to 220°C and lightly grease six 10cm tart tins.

2 Slice the tomatoes in half. Place 3 tomato halves in each tart tin, cut side up. Sprinkle the olives over. Spread the onion jam evenly on top. Place the pastry rounds on top and fold in the edges. Bake until the pastry is golden and cooked through, about 15 – 20 minutes.

3 Toss the rocket in a little lemon juice and olive oil to moisten.

4 Turn each tart out onto a serving plate and drape 2 anchovy fillets over each tart. Top with the rocket and Parmesan, drizzle with the balsamic vinegar and serve.

Tomatoes, olives and anchovies marry **PERFECTLY IN** THIS LIGHT STARTER

Pear-and-cardamom tart with vanilla-pod crème anglaise

RECIPE BY **KAREN SHORT** STYLING BY **HELENA ERASMUS** PHOTOGRAPH BY **GRAEME BORCHERS**

Serves 8 **EASY** 50 mins + 1 hr, to chill

THE FLAVOUR COMBINATIONS
200g cake flour
100g unsalted butter
30ml (2 tbsp) castor sugar
pinch salt
30ml (2 tbsp) chilled water

POACHED PEARS
500ml (2 cups) water
850g castor sugar
10 cardamom pods, cracked open
1 cinnamon stick
1 star anise
3 pears

FILLING
190g ground almonds
110g unsalted butter
130g castor sugar + extra, to sprinkle
3 eggs
15ml (1 tbsp) cocoa powder

VANILLA-POD CRÈME ANGLAISE
250ml (1 cup) milk
3 vanilla pods, split lengthways
3 egg yolks
50ml castor sugar

HOW TO DO IT

1 Preheat the oven to 180°C. Place the flour, 100g butter, 30ml (2 tbsp) castor sugar and salt in a food processor and blitz for 1 minute. Add the chilled water and pulse until the mixture comes together. Wrap the dough in cling film and refrigerate to chill, 30 minutes.

2 Roll the pastry out as thinly as possible and line a greased 25cm-round tart tin with the pastry. Refrigerate to chill for a further 30 minutes. Prick the base and blind-bake until the pastry is dry and cooked, about 10 – 15 minutes. Remove and allow to cool.

3 For the poached pears, combine the water, 850g castor sugar, cardamom, cinnamon stick and star anise in a large pot, and stir over low heat without boiling until the sugar has dissolved. Peel the pears, add them to the liquid, cover and simmer until soft, about 15 minutes. Remove from heat, cover the pot with greaseproof paper to keep the pears submerged, and leave to cool. Once cooled, remove the pears from the liquid and strain.

4 For the filling, place the ground almonds, 110g butter, 130g castor sugar, eggs and cocoa in a food processor and blend to form a thick paste. Carefully spoon and spread the mixture into the pastry case. Core and quarter the pears, slice them thickly and arrange in a fan over the top of the almond mixture. Bake for 20 minutes.

5 For the crème anglaise, scald the milk with the vanilla pod by bringing it to just below boiling point. Beat the egg yolks and 50ml castor sugar together, pour the warm milk over and mix well. Return to the pan and stir over low heat with a wooden spoon until the custard is thick enough to coat the back of the spoon. Do not allow to boil. Strain into a bowl and cover tightly with a sheet of greaseproof paper to prevent a skin from forming.

6 Remove the tart from the oven and sprinkle with the extra castor sugar. Return to the oven for a further 10 minutes. The tart is cooked when a skewer inserted into the centre comes out clean. Allow to cool slightly.

7 Serve sliced and drizzled with the vanilla crème anglaise.

COOK'S TIPS
This tart freezes well for up to 1 month. The pears can be substituted with apples.

Pumpkin, white chocolate and almond crumble pie

RECIPE AND STYLING BY **JACQUES ERASMUS** PHOTOGRAPH BY **MYBURGH DU PLESSIS**

Serves 4 – 6 **EASY** 1 hr

THE FLAVOUR COMBINATIONS
FILLING
500ml (2 cups) pumpkin purée/
cooked butternut, mashed
4 eggs
125g white chocolate, melted
15ml (1 tbsp) cake flour
2,5ml (½ tsp) vanilla extract
pinch salt

CRUMBLE
120g cake flour
90g flaked almonds
190g butter, melted
45ml (3 tbsp) sugar
pinch cinnamon
pinch nutmeg, freshly grated
pinch salt

white-chocolate shavings, to serve
vanilla ice cream, to serve (optional)

HOW TO DO IT

1 Preheat the oven to 180°C. For the filling, combine the pumpkin purée or mashed butternut and eggs in a bowl using a whisk. Mix in the melted chocolate, then fold in the 15ml (1 tbsp) flour, vanilla and salt. Once combined, spoon into a 20cm oven dish or into hollowed-out pumpkin or butternut shells.

2 For the crumble, combine all of the ingredients in a bowl and rub together with your fingers until well mixed.

3 Sprinkle the crumble over the filling and bake in the oven until golden and set, 35 – 40 minutes. Serve warm topped with white-chocolate shavings and a side of vanilla ice cream, if desired.

COOK'S TIP
When using hollowed-out pumpkins, reduce or increase the baking time, depending on the thickness of the pumpkins' flesh.

The combination of coffee and rose syrup is a match made in heaven and reminiscent of the Middle East, where coffee has its origins.

Coffee and rose-scented meringues

RECIPE BY **LEANDRI VAN DER WAT** STYLING BY **LEANDRI** AND **SELINE VAN DER WAT** PHOTOGRAPH BY **CURTIS GALLON**

Makes 20 **EASY** 1 hr 30 mins +
40 mins, to cool

THE FLAVOUR COMBINATIONS
200g (6 – 7) egg whites
pinch salt
140g demerara sugar
260g castor sugar
60ml (¼ cup) strong coffee
(brewed in an espresso maker
or a moka pot)
60g white sugar
40ml rose syrup

pistachio nuts, grated, to dust

HOW TO DO IT

1 Preheat the oven to 110°C. Place the egg whites, salt, demerara sugar and castor sugar in a glass bowl. Set the bowl over a pot of boiling water (don't allow the bottom of the bowl to touch the water). Stir the mixture with a spatula for 8 minutes exactly, making sure not to let the egg whites scramble. Remove from heat.

2 Beat the mixture with an electric beater until cool and the meringue is silky and shiny, about 10 minutes.

3 Meanwhile, heat the coffee and white sugar in a pot over medium-high heat until the mixture has reduced to a thick syrup, about 5 minutes.

4 Carefully fold the rose syrup and coffee syrup into the meringue mixture. Scoop onto a greased baking sheet (or you could line it with a silicone mat) and bake in the oven, 1 hour. Switch off the oven and leave the meringues to cool inside with the door closed, about 40 minutes. Dust with grated pistachio nuts to serve.

Mélange of winter roasted fruit in red wine on bread-and-butter puddings with vanilla-pod mascarpone

RECIPE AND STYLING BY **VICKY CREASE** PHOTOGRAPH BY **VANESSA LEWIS**

Serves 6 – 8 **EASY** 1 hr 10 mins

THE FLAVOUR COMBINATIONS
BREAD-AND-BUTTER PUDDINGS
25g butter + extra, to grease
8 thin slices white bread
10ml (2 tsp) sultanas
10ml (2 tsp) ground cinnamon
125ml (½ cup) smooth apricot jam
250ml (1 cup) milk
50ml double-thick cream
2 large eggs
45ml (3 tbsp) white sugar

FRUIT MÉLANGE
500ml (2 cups) red wine
125ml (½ cup) water
1 cinnamon stick
thick peel of 1 orange
200g sugar
2 medium pears, peeled and thinly sliced
45ml (3 tbsp) blueberries
250g strawberries
250g mascarpone
1 vanilla pod

icing sugar, to dust

HOW TO DO IT

1 Preheat the oven to 180°C. Grease individual pudding cups with butter.

2 For the puddings, cut the crusts off the bread and spread each slice with the butter, then cut each slice into four triangles. Arrange a layer of bread, buttered side up, in the bottom of each cup, sprinkle with the sultanas, cinnamon and a dollop each of apricot jam. Repeat the layers of bread and sultanas and finish with a layer of bread. Set aside.

3 Gently warm the milk and cream in a saucepan over low heat. Crack the eggs into a bowl, add 25ml (5 tsp) of the 45ml (3 tbsp) white sugar and whisk lightly until pale. Add the warm milk and cream to the egg mixture, stir to form a custard and strain this into a bowl.

4 Pour the custard over the puddings and sprinkle with the remaining white sugar. Bake until the custard has set and the tops are golden, 30 – 40 minutes.

5 For the mélange, combine the wine, water, cinnamon stick, orange peel and 200g sugar in a large, heavy-bottomed pot and bring to a gentle simmer. When it thickens slightly, add the fruit and poach, turning occasionally, about 30 minutes.

6 Place the mascarpone in a bowl. Cut the vanilla pod lengthways and scrape the seeds into the mascarpone, mixing thoroughly. Place a dollop of the mascarpone mixture on each pudding and finish off with 15ml (1 tbsp) fruit mélange on top of this. Dust with icing sugar and serve.

188

August

AS WINTER BEGINS TO (VERY SLOWLY) COME TO A MUCH-ANTICIPATED END, IT'S TIME TO CHANGE THINGS UP AND ADD INTRIGUE TO YOUR COOKING. STARTING OFF WITH A ZIPPY COCKTAIL, FOR MAINS AND DESSERTS WE'VE THROWN IN SOME FEISTY INGREDIENTS TO LIFT YOU OUT OF YOUR WINTER COMA – THINK GINGER, GRAPEFRUIT, SAFFRON, ROSE, LAVENDER, POMEGRANATE AND SAKE!

Japanese slipper

RECIPE AND STYLING BY **INGRID CASSON** PHOTOGRAPH BY **GRAEME BORCHERS**

Serves 1 **EASY** 5 mins

THE FLAVOUR COMBINATIONS
1 shot (25ml) melon liqueur
1 shot (25ml) Cointreau
1 shot (25ml) lime juice

HOW TO DO IT

1 Add all of the ingredients to a cocktail shaker and shake to combine. Serve in a martini glass.

Chilli crab with ginger

RECIPE AND STYLING BY **ANNA MONTALI** ASSISTED BY **NOMVUSELELO MNCUBE** PHOTOGRAPH BY **GRAEME BORCHERS**

Serves 4 **EASY** 30 mins

THE FLAVOUR COMBINATIONS
45ml (3 tbsp) fresh ginger, chopped
4 garlic cloves, peeled and crushed
2 red chillies, seeded
and finely chopped
20ml (4 tsp) sugar
10ml (2 tsp) sunflower oil
60ml (¼ cup) tomato sauce
60ml (¼ cup) tamarind paste
125ml (½ cup) water
juice of 1 lime
10 crab pieces, cooked

fresh coriander, to garnish

HOW TO DO IT

1 Pound the ginger, garlic, chillies and sugar in a pestle and mortar until you have a paste.

2 Heat the oil in a wok or large frying pan and gently fry the ginger paste for about 2 minutes. Add the tomato sauce, tamarind paste, water and lime juice and simmer briefly.

3 Add the crab pieces and heat through for about 5 minutes.

4 Serve the crab garnished with coriander, along with finger bowls, plenty of serviettes and mallets for cracking the claws.

Baby aubergine tempura with a sweet-chilli dipping sauce

RECIPE AND STYLING BY **VICKIE DE BEER** ASSISTED BY **JANA VAN SITTERT** AND **INEMARI RABIE** PHOTOGRAPH BY **LEE MALAN**

Serves 6 **EASY** 1 hr +
30 mins, to chill

THE FLAVOUR COMBINATIONS
TEMPURA
170g flour
30ml (2 tbsp) cornflour
pinch salt
375ml (1½ cups) sparkling water
vegetable oil, to deep-fry
**12 baby aubergines, quartered/
halved**

DIPPING SAUCE
**60g (about 4) long fresh red chillies,
trimmed**
1 garlic clove, peeled
180ml white vinegar
165g castor sugar
juice of 1 lime
30ml (2 tbsp) soya sauce

HOW TO DO IT

1 Place the flour, cornflour and salt in a mixing bowl. Add the sparkling water and whisk until the batter is smooth. Cover and refrigerate, 30 minutes.

2 For the sauce, halve and roughly chop 20g of the chillies. Seed and chop the remaining chillies.

3 Place the chillies, garlic and 60ml (¼ cup) of the white vinegar in a food processor and blend until finely chopped.

4 Place the chilli mixture, the remaining vinegar and the castor sugar in a large saucepan over low heat and cook, stirring, until the sugar dissolves, about 5 minutes.

5 Increase the heat to high and bring to a boil. Reduce the heat to medium and simmer, stirring occasionally, until the sauce thickens, 35 – 40 minutes.

6 Allow the sweet-chilli sauce to cool slightly before whisking in the lime juice and soya sauce.

7 Heat the oil in a large saucepan. Dip the aubergines in the batter and shake off the excess batter. Gently fry the aubergines in batches until golden, 5 – 7 minutes. Drain on paper towel. Serve warm with the sweet-chilli dipping sauce.

197

Garden pea soup with Parma ham breadsticks

RECIPE AND STYLING BY **ANNA MONTALI** PHOTOGRAPH BY **ROELENE PRINSLOO**

Serves 4 **EASY** 20 mins

THE FLAVOUR COMBINATIONS
45ml (3 tbsp) olive oil
1 large onion, peeled and
finely chopped
2 garlic cloves, peeled and
finely chopped
1kg fresh garden peas
1,2L beef stock, hot
30ml (2 tbsp) fresh flat-leaf
parsley, chopped
190ml fresh cream
salt and freshly ground black
pepper, to taste

8 thin grissini breadsticks, wrapped
in 8 slices Parma ham, to serve

HOW TO DO IT

1 Heat the olive oil in a saucepan over medium heat and sauté the onion and garlic, 1 – 2 minutes. Add the peas and sauté for 1 minute.

2 Pour in the stock and parsley and bring to a boil. Reduce the heat and allow to simmer, about 10 minutes.

3 Use a hand blender to blitz the soup until smooth. Add the cream and season to taste.

4 Serve hot topped with the Parma ham-wrapped grissini breadsticks.

Grapefruit-and-edamame salad with ginger-and-maple-syrup dressing

RECIPE AND STYLING BY **CLAIRE FERRANDI** ASSISTED BY **NOMVUSELELO MNCUBE** PHOTOGRAPH BY **DYLAN SWART**

Serves 4 **EASY** 15 mins

THE FLAVOUR COMBINATIONS
SALAD
150g edamame pods
120g sugar snap peas
2 grapefruits, peeled and sliced
150g radishes, finely sliced
30g white salad onions, peeled and
finely sliced lengthways
handful fresh mint leaves
handful fresh pea shoots

DRESSING
15ml (1 tbsp) maple syrup
1,5cm piece ginger, peeled
and grated
7,5ml (1½ tsp) water
30ml (2 tbsp) olive oil
juice of ½ lemon
7,5ml (1½ tsp) white vinegar
salt and freshly ground black
pepper, to taste

HOW TO DO IT

1 Bring a medium-sized saucepan of salted water to a boil. Blanch the edamame pods and sugar snap peas, 3 minutes. Drain the vegetables and discard the water. Remove the tough outer pods of the edamames and reserve the beans.

2 On a serving platter, arrange the edamame, sugar snap peas, grapefruit slices, sliced radishes and salad onions. Sprinkle with fresh mint leaves and pea shoots.

3 For the dressing, whisk all of the ingredients together and season to taste. Just before serving, dress the salad.

COOK'S TIP
Edamame beans are immature soya beans in the pod, and feature often in the cuisines of China, Japan, Indonesia, Korea and Hawaii. The pods can be found in the frozen-foods section of Asian supermarkets.

Quail ravioli with sherry cream

RECIPE AND STYLING BY **VICKIE DE BEER** PHOTOGRAPH BY **NEVILLE LOCKHART**

Serves 4 **EASY** 1 hr

THE FLAVOUR COMBINATIONS
RAVIOLI
240g cake flour
pinch salt
2 large eggs
30ml (2 tbsp) olive oil
30ml (2 tbsp) water

QUAILS
4 quails
25ml (5 tsp) olive oil
60g butter
4 sprigs fresh thyme
4 garlic cloves, peeled
15ml (1 tbsp) raisins
salt and freshly ground black
pepper, to taste

SHERRY CREAM
250ml (1 cup) fresh cream
1 fresh bay leaf
60ml (¼ cup) medium cream sherry

FILLING
2,5ml (½ tsp) ground cinnamon
pinch ground star anise
20g butter, melted
5ml (1 tsp) fresh thyme leaves

diced tomatoes, to garnish
fresh sage leaves, to garnish

HOW TO DO IT

1 Preheat the oven to 180°C. For the pasta, sift the flour and salt into a bowl.

2 Combine the eggs, 30ml (2 tbsp) olive oil and water in a separate bowl. Slowly add the liquid to the dry ingredients while incorporating all of the flour.

3 Knead the dough until smooth, wrap in cling film and set aside to rest, at least 30 minutes.

4 Place the quails on a roasting tray. Drizzle with the 25ml (5 tsp) olive oil and place the 60g butter under the skin of each breast. Insert a sprig of thyme, a garlic clove and the raisins into the cavity of each quail. Season to taste and roast in the oven, 15 – 20 minutes. Remove and allow to cool.

5 For the sherry cream, combine the cream, bay leaf and sherry in a small saucepan over medium heat. Allow to reduce by half or until the mixture coats the back of the spoon, about 10 minutes.

6 Cut the legs off the quails and set aside until needed. Strip the rest of the meat from each carcass and place in a small bowl. Add all of the filling ingredients and season to taste.

7 Using a pasta machine, roll the pasta dough out into thin sheets, up to the number-6 setting on the machine. Cut the pasta into equal-sized squares of about 5cm x 5cm. Spoon 15ml (1 tbsp) filling onto a square and cover with another. Seal the pockets by pinching the sides with your fingers and ensuring that no excess air is trapped inside. Just before serving, cook for 3 minutes in salted, boiling water.

8 Serve the ravioli with 2 quail legs each, spoon over the sherry cream and garnish with tomatoes and sage.

COOK'S TIP
You can substitute the quail with about 300g cooked whole chicken.

Ravioli is a wonderful 'container' for a myriad delightful fillings. You will need a pasta machine for this recipe – and remember that the fillings cannot be too watery, or they will seep out during the cooking process.

Breaded rack of lamb

RECIPE BY **TOMI MILLER** AND **ELIZABETH DOWNES** STYLING BY **SARAH DALL** PHOTOGRAPH BY **BRUCE TUCK**

Serves 4 **EASY** 30 mins

THE FLAVOUR COMBINATIONS
1 medium (about 1,5kg) rack of lamb
3,75ml (¾ tsp) salt
2,5ml (½ tsp) freshly ground
black pepper
15ml (1 tbsp) vegetable oil
30ml (2 tbsp) Dijon mustard
10ml (2 tsp) garlic, peeled
and minced
60ml (¼ cup) seasoned breadcrumbs
2,5ml (½ tsp) ground cumin
15ml (1 tbsp) Parmesan, grated

green beans with orange zest and
red-onion slices, to serve
lemon wedges, to garnish

HOW TO DO IT

1 Preheat the oven to 230°C. Season the lamb well on all sides with the salt and pepper. Heat a medium skillet over high heat and, when hot, add the vegetable oil. Right before the oil begins to smoke, add the lamb and brown on all sides, about 6 minutes. Transfer to a plate and set aside to cool slightly before proceeding.

2 Mix the mustard and garlic together and spread over all sides of the lamb. Combine the breadcrumbs, cumin and Parmesan in a shallow bowl. Press the rack of lamb into the breadcrumb mixture, coating it evenly on all sides. Place the lamb on a baking sheet and cook in the oven, 12 – 15 minutes for medium-rare.

3 Remove from oven and allow to rest, 5 – 10 minutes, before carving. Serve with a side of the green beans and lemon wedges for squeezing.

Deconstructed mushroom-and-butternut lasagne with lavender-infused butter

RECIPE AND STYLING BY **THULISA MARTINS** PHOTOGRAPH BY **DYLAN SWART**

Serves 4 **EASY** 45 mins

THE FLAVOUR COMBINATIONS
pinch salt
15ml (1 tbsp) olive oil
500g dry lasagne sheets
50g pine nuts, roasted
10g Parmesan, shaved
sea salt and freshly ground black
pepper, to taste

FILLING
50g salted butter
300g button mushrooms, sliced
100ml double-thick cream
600g butternut, peeled, seeded,
thinly sliced and boiled until soft

BUTTER
50g salted butter
10ml (2 tsp) lavender flowers,
finely chopped
small handful fresh sage, chopped

small handful fresh lavender sprigs,
to garnish

HOW TO DO IT

1 Boil enough water to cover the lasagne sheets in a large saucepan over medium heat. Add the salt, olive oil and lasagne sheets one at a time, and boil until al dente, 10 – 15 minutes.

2 For the creamy mushroom filling, melt the 50g butter in a saucepan over medium heat. Add the mushrooms and fry, 5 minutes. Add the cream and cook while stirring, 1 minute. Set aside.

3 For the lavender-infused butter, heat a separate saucepan over low heat and melt the 50g butter. Once the butter starts to sizzle, add the lavender and sage. Remove from heat and set aside to infuse, 15 – 20 minutes.

4 To assemble, layer the lasagne sheets, mushrooms and butternut slices in a bowl. Drizzle with the lavender butter and sprinkle with pine nuts and Parmesan shavings. Season to taste and garnish with fresh lavender. Serve while still warm.

Sake-and-mint melon balls

RECIPE AND STYLING BY **LISA CLARK** PHOTOGRAPH BY **BRUCE TUCK**

Serves 4 **EASY** 20 mins

THE FLAVOUR COMBINATIONS
**1 winter/honeydew melon, halved
and seeded
80g sugar
100ml water
zest of 2 limes
45ml (3 tbsp) castor sugar
15ml (1 tbsp) sake
juice of 1 lime
4 fresh mint leaves, finely sliced
½ red chilli, seeded and finely sliced**

HOW TO DO IT

1 Preheat the oven to 100°C. Using a melon baller, make as many balls as you can from the melon. Set aside.

2 Place the sugar and water in a small saucepan and bring to a boil. Boil without stirring until you have a syrup, about 3 minutes.

3 Mix together the lime zest and castor sugar and place on a small baking sheet. Bake in the oven until the mixture has dried out, about 3 – 5 minutes.

4 Mix together the sugar syrup, sake, lime juice, mint leaves and chilli. Place the melon balls in a large bowl, pour over the syrup and sprinkle with the lime-zest sugar to serve.

209

Steamed apple surprise

RECIPE AND STYLING BY **KANYACILLA HUNT** PHOTOGRAPH BY **NEIL CORDER**

Serves 8 **EASY** 45 mins + 2 hrs, to steam

THE FLAVOUR COMBINATIONS
**500g Granny Smith apples,
quartered and cored
zest and juice of 1 lemon
50g butter
50ml caramel sugar
5ml (1 tsp) ground cinnamon**

BATTER
**125g butter
125g treacle sugar
60ml (¼ cup) maple syrup
100g bran-rich self-raising flour
200g oats
10ml (2 tsp) ground cinnamon
pinch salt
2 jumbo eggs, beaten**

custard, to serve

HOW TO DO IT

1 Grease and line the bottom of a 1,5L pudding basin with baking paper. Cut a baking paper lid to size. Pleat the baking paper across the middle and butter well.

2 Cut each apple quarter into 2 – 3 slices. Toss in the freshly squeezed lemon juice to prevent discolouring.

3 Place the 50g butter, caramel sugar and 5ml (1 tsp) ground cinnamon in a heavy-bottomed saucepan and heat until it starts to bubble. Add the apples and cook for no longer than 30 seconds – 1 minute. Turn off the heat and add the lemon zest. Transfer the apples to a separate bowl and set aside.

4 For the batter, use the same saucepan the apples were cooked in to melt the 125g butter, treacle sugar and maple syrup. Set aside to cool.

5 Sift the flour into a medium-sized mixing bowl and return the husks to the bowl of sifted flour. Add the oats, 10ml (2 tsp) cinnamon and salt, and stir to mix.

6 Make a well in the centre of the dry ingredients and pour in the lukewarm butter mixture, as well as the eggs. Mix the eggs well into the butter mixture before incorporating the dry ingredients from the sides. Mix to a smooth batter.

7 Spread two thirds of the pudding mixture on the bottom and sides of the pudding basin. The batter will be runny. Spoon the apple mixture into the centre and cover with the remaining pudding mixture. Cover with the paper lid and tie securely with string. Seal with a damp cloth drenched with flour. Tie the ends on top of the pudding basin for easy handling, then steam for 2 hours.

8 Allow the pudding to settle, 10 – 15 minutes, before turning it out. Serve with custard.

COOK'S TIP
You can substitute the caramel sugar with demerara sugar and treacle sugar with muscovado sugar. Bran-rich self-raising flour is available at health shops.

Apart from tasting simply superb, this steamed pudding distinguishes itself from other puddings with its wonderfully high fibre content. It provides just over 4g fibre per portion, which is pretty good going for a pudding!

Coconut-and-lemongrass panna cotta with pomegranate syrup

RECIPE AND STYLING BY **LISA CLARK** PHOTOGRAPH BY **BRUCE TUCK**

Makes 6 **EASY** 40 mins +
setting time

THE FLAVOUR COMBINATIONS
500ml (2 cups) coconut milk
50ml sugar
2 lemongrass stalks, bruised
20ml (4 tsp)/7 leaves gelatine
40ml water
250ml (1 cup) fresh cream, whipped
30ml (2 tbsp) pomegranate rubies
45ml (3 tbsp) sugar syrup
(see 'Cook's tip')

fresh coconut shavings, to serve

HOW TO DO IT

1 Scald the coconut milk in a saucepan with the sugar and lemongrass. Set aside and allow to infuse for 15 minutes. Once the milk has a lemon flavour, remove the lemongrass.

2 Sprinkle the gelatine in the water, carefully dissolve in the microwave and add to the warm coconut milk. If using leaf gelatine, first soak the leaves in cold water until softened and then add to the coconut milk. Refrigerate until slightly thickened, stirring occasionally.

3 Fold in the cream, pour into 6 greased dariole moulds and refrigerate to set.

4 Stir the pomegranate rubies into the sugar syrup and allow to infuse while the panna cotta is setting.

5 To serve, turn each panna cotta out onto a plate, top with the pomegranate syrup and garnish with coconut shavings.

COOK'S TIP
To make sugar syrup, place equal quantities of sugar and water in a saucepan and boil without stirring until you have a syrup consistency, about 3 minutes.

Mile-high chocolate-brownie flapjack stack with pretzel brittle and peanut-butter sauce

RECIPE, STYLING AND PHOTOGRAPH BY **KATELYN WILLIAMS** ASSISTED BY **ANTONIO ALLEGRA**

Makes 8 – 10 **EASY** 45 mins

THE FLAVOUR COMBINATIONS
FLAPJACKS
200g white sugar
200g cake flour
100g cocoa powder
7,5ml (1½ tsp) baking powder
pinch salt
1 egg
125ml (½ cup) buttermilk
5ml (1 tsp) vanilla extract
160ml black coffee, hot
30ml (2 tbsp) smooth peanut butter
60g butter, melted

BRITTLE
100g salted pretzels
200g white sugar
60ml (¼ cup) water

SAUCE
240g creamy peanut butter
60ml (¼ cup) peanut oil
45ml (3 tbsp) icing sugar, sifted
pinch salt

HOW TO DO IT

1 For the chocolate-brownie flapjacks, mix the dry ingredients – the sugar, flour, cocoa, baking powder and salt – together in a bowl.

2 In a separate bowl, whisk the egg, buttermilk and vanilla extract, then add to the dry ingredients.

3 In a separate bowl, combine the coffee, peanut butter and butter and add to the mixture. The mixture should be of a dropping consistency.

4 Heat a non-stick pan over medium heat and grease well. Drop tablespoonfuls of the batter into the pan. When bubbles start to form on the surface, flip the flapjacks over and cook on the other side, 1 – 2 minutes. Repeat with the remaining batter.

5 For the pretzel brittle, scatter the pretzels on a silicone mat or baking paper. Place the sugar in a saucepan with the water and heat gently over medium heat until the sugar has dissolved. Bring to a boil, then simmer until the sugar turns into a deep caramel. Remove from heat and pour over the pretzels. Allow to set before breaking into pieces.

6 For the peanut-butter sauce, combine all of the ingredients in a bowl. Stir until smooth.

7 Serve the flapjacks piled high on top of each other, sprinkled with pieces of brittle and drizzled with peanut-butter sauce.

THE MONTH OF

September

SPRING IS HERE AND IT'S TIME TO INJECT NEW LIFE INTO EVERYTHING THAT COMES OUT OF YOUR KITCHEN! BOTH THE MOOD AND THE WEATHER ALL GET A LITTLE LIGHTER, SO WE'VE OPTED TO ALSO LIGHTEN UP WHAT YOU EAT – THINK EVERYTHING FROM FRESH VEGETABLES, SPRING CHICKENS AND FISH TO TASTY TARTS AND PIES WITH A TWIST

Rose, pink pepper and Champagne slush

RECIPE AND STYLING BY **JACQUES ERASMUS** PHOTOGRAPH BY **MYBURGH DU PLESSIS**

Serves 6 EASY 10 mins

THE FLAVOUR COMBINATIONS

150 ice cubes
450ml Champagne/sparkling wine, chilled
200ml rose syrup (available at speciality stores) + extra, if needed
5ml (1 tsp) pink peppercorns + extra, to garnish
pinch salt
15ml (1 tbsp) lemon juice
2 garden roses (organic and unsprayed), petals removed

HOW TO DO IT

1 Place all of the ingredients in a liquidiser and blend until smooth. Add more rose syrup to adjust the sweetness.

2 Spoon into glasses and serve garnished with pink peppercorns.

Slow-roasted beetroot and butternut with caramelised pumpkin seeds

RECIPE AND STYLING BY **TINA MARITZ** PHOTOGRAPH BY **ANDREA VAN DER SPUY**

Serves 6 **EASY** 1 hr + cooling time

THE FLAVOUR COMBINATIONS

1kg beetroot, cleaned
60ml (¼ cup) olive oil
1 large butternut, sliced
30ml (2 tbsp) honey
30ml (2 tbsp) treacle sugar
100g pumpkin seeds
100g chevin
50g crimson microherbs, to garnish

HOW TO DO IT

1 Preheat the oven to 180°C. Place the beetroot on a baking tray, drizzle with half of the olive oil and roast until tender, about 1 hour.

2 Place the sliced butternut on a baking tray, rub with the remaining olive oil and bake alongside the beetroot, 40 minutes.

3 Remove the beetroot and butternut from the oven and allow to cool to room temperature.

4 In a non-stick frying pan over medium heat, caramelise the honey and sugar, about 10 minutes, then add the pumpkin seeds. Pour the hot mixture onto baking paper and leave to cool completely before breaking into shards.

5 Arrange the beetroot, butternut and chevin on a platter, sprinkle with the pumpkin-seed shards and garnish with crimson microherbs.

Corn, feta and herb fritters with creamed avocado

RECIPE AND STYLING BY **ILLANIQUE VAN ASWEGEN** PHOTOGRAPH BY **ADEL FERREIRA** ASSISTED BY **JÖMERI MOUTON**

Makes 16 – 20 EASY 45 mins

THE FLAVOUR COMBINATIONS
FRITTERS

500ml (2 cups) corn kernels, cooked
1 whole spring onion, thinly sliced
15ml (1 tbsp) fresh basil,
finely chopped
15ml (1 tbsp) fresh dill, chopped
20ml (4 tsp) sweet-chilli sauce
1 feta round, crumbled
120g cake flour
15ml (1 tbsp) sugar
5ml (1 tsp) fine salt
5ml (1 tsp) baking powder
5ml (1 tsp) paprika
5ml (1 tsp) dried sage
250g plain yoghurt
2 large eggs
olive oil, to fry

CREAMED AVOCADO

3 avocados, peeled and pips removed
15ml (1 tbsp) lemon juice
30ml (2 tbsp) balsamic vinegar
salt and white pepper, to taste
Tabasco sauce, to taste (optional)

cracked black pepper, to serve
grilled vine tomatoes, to serve
maple-glazed crispy bacon, to serve

HOW TO DO IT

1 For the fritters, combine the corn, spring onion, basil, dill, sweet-chilli sauce and feta in a mixing bowl.

2 Combine the flour, sugar, salt, baking powder, paprika and dried sage in a separate bowl and whisk in the plain yoghurt and eggs until smooth. Stir in the vegetable mixture and refrigerate for up to 1 hour before cooking.

3 For the creamed avocado, blend the avocados, lemon juice and vinegar together. Season with salt and white pepper. Add a few drops of Tabasco sauce if you like it a little spicy.

4 Heat a non-stick pan over medium heat and add a drizzle of olive oil. Drop tablespoons of the fritter batter into the pan and cook until golden and crisp, 2 – 3 minutes on each side. Keep them warm under a clean tea towel while you cook the remaining fritters.

5 Serve the fritters with creamed avocado and lots of cracked black pepper. They're perfect with grilled vine tomatoes and crispy bacon.

Garden herb salad with goat's cheese wontons, fresh cherries and a blueberry dressing

RECIPE BY **KAREN SHORT** STYLING BY **HELENA ERASMUS** PHOTOGRAPH BY **GRAEME BORCHERS**

Serves 4 **EASY** 30 mins

THE FLAVOUR COMBINATIONS
SALAD

**handful assorted fresh
herbs, chopped
100g soft goat's cheese
16 wonton wrappers (available at
Chinese supermarkets)
water, to brush
oil, to deep-fry
handful fresh assorted salad leaves
10ml (2 tsp) olive oil**

BLUEBERRY DRESSING

**250g blueberries, fresh or tinned
1cm fresh ginger, peeled and
thinly sliced
20ml (4 tsp) castor sugar
juice of 1 lemon
250ml (1 cup) water
5ml (1 tsp) sesame oil
salt and freshly ground black
pepper, to taste**

250g cherries, to serve

HOW TO DO IT

1 Mix the herbs with the goat's cheese and place 5ml (1 tsp) mixture in the centre of each of the wonton wrappers. Brush the edges with a little water, then bring together the sides and seal to form parcels.

2 Heat the oil in a deep-fryer or deep pot to 180°C. Carefully place the wrappers in the oil and fry until golden brown. Drain on paper towel.

3 Mix the assorted salad leaves with the olive oil.

4 For the dressing, place half of the berries (drained if using tinned) in a pan with the ginger, sugar, lemon juice and water. Simmer for 5 minutes over medium heat, stirring to dissolve the sugar. Leave to cool and add the sesame oil and remaining berries. Season to taste.

5 To serve, arrange the wontons and cherries on the salad and drizzle the dressing over.

COOK'S TIP
This dish can be served as a starter or main meal. Buy the best goat's cheese you can – it makes all the difference.

*A light, but flavourful salad! The crunchy, oozing
wontons and rich, fruity dressing ring of dying winter
days, while perfectly paving the way to spring.*

Fennel, coriander and lemon salad

RECIPE AND STYLING BY **ANNA MONTALI** ASSISTED BY **NOMVUSELELO MNCUBE** PHOTOGRAPH BY **ROELENE PRINSLOO**

Serves 5 EASY 5 mins

THE FLAVOUR COMBINATIONS

4 fennel bulbs, thinly sliced
200g fresh coriander, leaves only
80ml ($^1/_3$ cup) olive oil
zest and juice of 1 lemon
15ml (1 tbsp) wholegrain mustard
salt and freshly ground black
pepper, to taste

HOW TO DO IT

1 Place the fennel and coriander in a bowl and toss to combine.

2 Mix together the remaining ingredients, season to taste and pour over the fennel and coriander to serve.

Hay-smoked stuffed baby chicken, grilled vegetable medley and honey-whisky marinade

RECIPE AND STYLING BY **DIRK GIESELMANN** PHOTOGRAPH BY **GRAEME WYLLIE**

Serves 4 EASY 1 hr

THE FLAVOUR COMBINATIONS
large bunch clean, dry hay

MARINADE
10ml (2 tsp) honey
10ml (2 tsp) teriyaki sauce
30ml (2 tbsp) bourbon whisky
zest and juice of 1 lemon
20ml (4 tsp) olive oil
salt and allspice, to taste
small handful fresh rosemary leaves
small handful fresh thyme leaves
small handful fresh sage leaves

2 baby chickens, deboned

VEGETABLE MEDLEY
1 small butternut,
peeled and seeded
1 garlic head
4 shallots
fruity extra-virgin olive oil, to taste
salt, to taste
150g white grapes
2 small bell peppers
200g green beans, blanched
100g chickpeas, cooked
salt and freshly ground black
pepper, to taste

STUFFING
1 red bell pepper
200g mozzarella
pinch freshly ground
Szechwan pepper, to taste
1 preserved lemon, chopped
small handful fresh basil leaves

PESTO
200g fresh flat-leaf parsley,
finely chopped
100g pumpkin seeds
200ml olive oil

fresh baguette, roasted, to serve

HOW TO DO IT

1 Light your braai and soak the hay in water.

2 For the marinade, whisk together all of the ingredients in a bowl. Place the deboned chickens in the marinade and set aside.

3 For the vegetable medley, wrap the butternut, garlic and shallots individually in foil, drizzle with extra-virgin olive oil and season with salt. When the flames are out, add the wrapped vegetables to the ashes. They will need 15 – 20 minutes to cook in their own juices. Once they are cooked, allow to rest in the foil. Peel the grapes, cut them in two, seed and set aside.

4 For the chicken stuffing, roast the red bell pepper on the grill until the skin is black. Place the pepper in a bowl, cover with cling film and set aside to sweat, 10 minutes. Peel the skin off, seed the pepper and cut into large strips lengthways. Slice up the mozzarella.

5 Lie the chickens, legs towards you, on a board. Season with Szechwan pepper and sprinkle over the preserved lemon. Place a layer of pepper, mozzarella and basil in the middle, roll them up tight and tie with kitchen string to retain their shape. Season lightly and place on the braai over medium heat. The chickens will need at least 30 minutes, turning halfway.

6 For the pesto, squeeze the flesh out of 4 of the garlic cloves (from the roasted garlic head) and add to the parsley and pumpkin seeds. Season with salt and pepper and grind in a pestle and mortar. Work them well together by adding the 200ml olive oil a little at a time. Fresh roasted garlic is just delicious – spread the remaining cloves over the roasted baguette.

7 After the chicken has cooked for 15 minutes, roast the 2 small bell peppers and the precooked butternut on the grill. Add the grapes, beans and chickpeas to the roasted shallot parcels and place in a corner of the braai to heat up before serving seasoned with salt and pepper.

8 Once the chickens are cooked, take the hay out of the water and put it on the braai. Lay the chickens on top to smoke, 3 – 4 minutes. Remove from the hay, cut off the string and carve. Dress with the vegetables and serve with the pesto and a roasted garlic baguette.

This is a wonderful way to use the first and quite aggressive energy of the braai to cook vegetables like potatoes, squash and beetroot, protected by foil. Actually, it's a good mix of French techniques and the South African lifestyle.

Sustainably farmed kabeljou with guava achar, spring salad and ciabatta toast

RECIPE AND STYLING BY **CLAIRE FERRANDI** ASSISTED BY **NOMVUSELELO MNCUBE** PHOTOGRAPH BY **GRAEME WYLLIE**

Serves 4 EASY 45 mins

THE FLAVOUR COMBINATIONS
GUAVA ACHAR
400g (about 4) fresh guavas
1 green chilli, halved lengthways and seeded
22,5ml (1½ tbsp) garam masala spice
60ml (¼ cup) white spirit vinegar
5ml (1 tsp) salt
1 fresh (or dried) bay leaf
small handful fresh dill, roughly chopped

DRESSING
30ml (2 tbsp) white wine vinegar
juice of ½ lemon
½ garlic clove, peeled and crushed
5ml (1 tsp) Dijon mustard
60ml (¼ cup) olive oil
10ml (2 tsp) water
salt and freshly ground black pepper, to taste

GUAVAS
2 guavas, cut into wedges
15ml (1 tbsp) olive oil

TOAST
100g butter
15ml (1 tbsp) olive oil
½ ciabatta loaf, sliced
salt, to taste

FISH
30ml (2 tbsp) olive oil
100g butter
600g farmed kabeljou (or other sustainable firm white fish), cut into 4 portions
zest and juice of 1 lemon
15ml (1 tbsp) fresh dill, roughly chopped
15ml (1 tbsp) fresh flat-leaf parsley, roughly chopped

SPRING SALAD
2 avocados, halved and chopped
5 (about 150g) mini cucumbers (or ½ large cucumber), shaved into ribbons using a vegetable peeler
60g baby herb salad leaves
2 large carrots, peeled and shaved into ribbons using a vegetable peeler (optional)
2 radishes, finely sliced (optional)

HOW TO DO IT

1 For the achar, bring a large pot of water to a boil. Add the whole guavas and cook, 20 minutes.

2 While the guavas are boiling, mix together the chilli, masala, white spirit vinegar, salt, bay leaf and dill in a bowl.

3 Allow the guavas to cool a little, about 10 minutes. Slice some into quarters and some in half. Mix the cut guavas with the vinegar mixture, mashing some of the guava flesh.

4 For the dressing, whisk together the white wine vinegar, lemon juice, garlic, mustard, olive oil and water in a small bowl. Season to taste and set aside.

5 To chargrill the guavas, heat a griddle pan or braai over high heat. Brush the guavas with the oil and chargrill, about 1 minute on each side. Set aside.

6 For the toast, if braaiing, melt the 100g butter, mix with the 15ml (1 tbsp) oil and brush over the ciabatta slices. Toast on the braai over hot coals, 1 minute per side. If making the toast on a stove, heat the butter and olive oil in a large griddle pan over high heat. Toast the slices in batches, about 1 minute per side. Sprinkle with salt to taste and set aside.

7 For the fish, if braaiing, melt the 30ml (2 tbsp) olive oil and 100g butter together. Brush over the fish and braai the fish over hot coals, about 3 minutes per side. If cooking the fish on the stove, melt the olive oil and butter over high heat in a large frying pan. Fry the fish in batches, 3 minutes per side. Once the fish is cooked, squeeze over some lemon juice, sprinkle with the lemon zest, dill and parsley, and season to taste.

8 Toss the salad ingredients in the dressing and arrange on four plates or a large serving platter. Either cut the fish into smaller portions or serve as larger portions and arrange alongside the salad, together with the chargrilled guavas, guava achar and ciabatta toast.

231

White bean and baby-marrow burgers with cashew mayo and a sprout salad

RECIPE AND STYLING **CLAIRE FERRANDI** ASSISTED BY **NOMVUSELELO MNCUBE** PHOTOGRAPH BY **DYLAN SWART**

Serves 4 EASY 15 – 30 mins

THE FLAVOUR COMBINATIONS
BURGERS
½ red onion, peeled and finely chopped
1 x 400g tin cannellini beans, drained
30ml (2 tbsp) flaxseeds
30ml (2 tbsp) chia seeds
30ml (2 tbsp) ground almonds
5ml (1 tsp) smoked paprika
zest of 1 lemon
4 baby marrows, grated
30g sunflower seeds
salt and freshly ground black pepper, to taste

MAYO
100g cashews, soaked for 10 minutes in boiling water, drained and water discarded
30ml (2 tbsp) water
15ml (1 tbsp) Dijon mustard
juice of ½ lemon
1 garlic clove, peeled and crushed
10ml (2 tsp) white spirit vinegar

4 burger buns, halved and toasted
handful lettuce leaves
1 avocado, peeled, pitted and sliced lengthways
2 tomatoes, sliced
1 red onion, peeled and sliced into rings
handful sprouts of your choice
lemon wedges, to squeeze

HOW TO DO IT

1 Prepare a braai to grill the burgers over medium-high heat.

2 For the burger patties, place all of the ingredients – except the baby marrows, sunflower seeds and seasoning – in a blender and blitz until just smooth. Remove from blender and stir in the grated baby marrows and sunflower seeds. Season well to taste.

3 Divide the burger mixture into 4 and shape into patties. Grill on the braai until slightly charred, 3 – 4 minutes.

4 For the vegan cashew mayo, place all of the ingredients in a blender and blitz until smooth. Season to taste.

5 To assemble the burgers, place a dollop of mayo on each burger-bun half. Top with some lettuce, a patty, avocado slices, tomato slices, red-onion slices and sprouts. Close the burgers and serve with lemon wedges for squeezing.

vegan

Key-lime pies with a twist

RECIPE AND STYLING BY **ANNA MONTALI** PHOTOGRAPH BY **GRAEME BORCHERS**

Serves 6 EASY 1 hr 20 mins

THE FLAVOUR COMBINATIONS

100g pecan nuts
45ml (3 tbsp) castor sugar
240g (2 cups) cake flour
80g butter, cubed
1 large egg, lightly beaten
5ml (1 tsp) vanilla seeds
icing sugar, to dust

FILLING

4 large egg yolks
170g castor sugar
125ml (½ cup) lime juice
100g mascarpone
125ml (½ cup) fresh cream, whipped
50ml lime zest + extra, to serve

HOW TO DO IT

1 For the pie crust, pulse the nuts a few times in a food processor. Add the sugar and flour and then pulse again until finely ground.

2 Add the butter and continue to pulse until the mixture resembles fine breadcrumbs. Add the egg and vanilla and pulse until you have firmer dough. Wrap in cling film and refrigerate, about 40 minutes.

3 Preheat the oven to 180°C and lightly grease six loose-bottomed tart tins.

4 With your fingertips, press the pastry evenly over the bases and up the sides of the tart tins. Blind-bake until the pastry is cooked through and golden, about 10 minutes. Allow to cool completely.

5 For the filling, whisk the egg yolks and sugar over a double boiler until smooth and thick. Add one third of the lime juice and continue to whisk vigorously. Repeat until all of the juice is used and the mixture has thickened.

6 Gently fold in the mascarpone, cream and zest. Pour the filling into the cases and bake, 20 minutes. Switch off the oven and leave to cool with the door ajar.

7 Remove the pies from the tins, dust with the icing sugar, sprinkle with extra lime zest and serve.

Oreo-and-strawberry white-chocolate tart

RECIPE AND STYLING BY **NOMVUSELELO MNCUBE** PHOTOGRAPH BY **DYLAN SWART**

Serves 8 – 10 **EASY** 1 hr 15 mins +
4 hrs or overnight, to set

THE FLAVOUR COMBINATIONS
2 x 176g packets Oreo biscuits
100g butter, melted

COULIS
125ml (½ cup) water
2,5ml (½ tsp) vanilla essence
130g castor sugar
300g strawberries, hulled and halved

FILLING
150ml fresh cream
300g white chocolate, melted
5 strawberries, hulled and halved

HOW TO DO IT

1 Grease a 36cm x 13cm tart tin. Place the Oreos in a food processor and pulse to a fine crumb. Pour into a mixing bowl, add the melted butter and stir to combine. Press the biscuit mixture into the tart tin to form a crust. Refrigerate to chill, about 1 hour.

2 For the coulis, add the water, vanilla essence and castor sugar to a saucepan and bring to a boil, without stirring, 15 minutes. Add the 300g strawberries and cook until soft, 10 minutes. Purée the mixture and set aside at room temperature to cool, about 20 minutes.

3 For the filling, heat the cream until just before boiling point. Mix the melted chocolate and cream and stir until smooth and well combined. Allow to cool for a further 10 minutes.

4 Remove the base from the fridge and pour in the chocolate-and-cream mixture until about two thirds full. Pour over 80ml (1/3 cup) coulis and swirl using a fork. Top with the halved strawberries and refrigerate to set, at least 4 hours or overnight. Serve with a side of the leftover coulis for pouring.

Biltong, salted almond and honey nougat with dried olives

RECIPE AND STYLING BY **JACQUES ERASMUS** PHOTOGRAPH BY **MYBURGH DU PLESSIS**

Makes 12 EASY 30 mins + cooling time

THE FLAVOUR COMBINATIONS

50g biltong dust + extra, to serve
250ml (1 cup) honey
645g sugar
125ml (½ cup) water
3 egg whites
75g icing sugar
120g salted almonds
150g pitted soft, dried olives (replace with dried prunes for a sweeter version)
10ml (2 tsp) coriander seeds, crushed

HOW TO DO IT

1 Prepare a large baking tray by greasing and scattering with the fine biltong dust.

2 Combine the honey, sugar and water in a saucepan over low heat and heat slowly until dissolved and starting to boil.

3 Place the egg whites in a mixer and whisk to soft peaks. Add the icing sugar in 3 batches and continue to whisk slowly while the syrup is boiling.

4 Boil the syrup over medium heat until it reaches 158°C on a sugar thermometer. Carefully remove the syrup from the heat and allow to reach 145°C. Slowly pour the hot syrup, little by little, into the egg whites, while whisking continuously. When all of the syrup has been added, reduce the mixer speed to low and whisk for a further 5 minutes until the mixture is slightly cooled. Fold in the nuts and dried olives.

5 Spoon the mixture onto the biltong dust, sprinkle with coriander seeds and gently fold the nougat several times to marble the biltong into the nougat. Allow to rest until cool. Cut into slices and serve sprinkled with extra biltong dust. Store in an airtight container – this is best served within 5 days.

Coconut-and-lime popsicles

RECIPE AND STYLING BY **ILLANIQUE VAN ASWEGEN** PHOTOGRAPH BY **ADEL FERREIRA** ASSISTED BY **JASMARI FERREIRA**

Makes 12 **EASY** 20 mins + 4 hrs or overnight, to freeze

THE FLAVOUR COMBINATIONS
250ml (1 cup) coconut milk
250ml (1 cup) coconut cream
250ml (1 cup) condensed milk
50g coconut, grated
seeds of ½ vanilla pod
zest of 1½ limes
juice of 1 lime
60g coconut shavings

HOW TO DO IT
1 Heat the coconut milk, coconut cream and condensed milk in a saucepan over medium heat, about 2 minutes.

2 Stir in the grated coconut, vanilla seeds, lime zest and juice. Pour the mixture into popsicle moulds and freeze for 1 hour.

3 Push wooden popsicle sticks into the centre of the moulds, top with the coconut shavings and freeze for at least another 3 hours or overnight.

COOK'S TIP
Replace the lime with orange- or lemon zest for alternative flavours.

240

THE MONTH OF *October*

A BOO-TIFUL PLATTER OF GOODIES – GREAT FOR
ENTERTAINING AT THAT HALLOWEEN CELEBRATION OR
FOR A FAB LUNCH OR DINNER PARTY WITH MATES.
LIGHT, DELICIOUS AND SUPER-IMPRESSIVE – IT'S TIME
TO EAT, DRINK AND BE SCARY!

Black-tooth cocktail

RECIPE BY **LIAM TOMLIN** PHOTOGRAPH BY **BRUCE TUCK**

Makes 4 – 6 **EASY** 10 mins

THE FLAVOUR COMBINATIONS
440ml Guinness
1 bottle Champagne/sparkling wine
30ml (1 shot) black sambuca/or
black food colouring (optional)

HOW TO DO IT

1 Chill the Guinness and Champagne or sparkling wine very well. Divide the Guinness among your Champagne flutes.

2 Top up with bubbly, then add a drop of black sambuca or food colouring. Serve immediately.

COOK'S TIP
Place plastic eyes, spiders or other scary bits at the base of each glass before pouring in the drink.

Chilled cucumber soup

RECIPE BY **HOPE TSHABANGU** AND **LERATO SHILAKOE** PHOTOGRAPH BY **DYLAN SWART**

Serves 2 **EASY** 10 mins

THE FLAVOUR COMBINATIONS
**1 cucumber, plus extra slices
to serve
2 celery sticks
salt and freshly ground black
pepper, to taste
ice cubes, to serve
fresh flat-leaf parsley, to garnish**

HOW TO DO IT

1 Chop the cucumber and celery into cubes, add to a blender, season and liquidise.

2 Serve the soup with ice and garnish with a slice of cucumber and some parsley.

Fresh asparagus topped with garlic breadcrumbs and eggs

RECIPE BY **SUSAN GREIG** STYLING BY **ANNA MONTALI** PHOTOGRAPH BY **GRAEME BORCHERS**

Serves 8 **EASY** 10 mins

THE FLAVOUR COMBINATIONS
80g butter, melted
30ml (2 tbsp) runny honey
2 garlic cloves, peeled and crushed
120g stale breadcrumbs
1kg fresh asparagus, trimmed
2 large eggs, hard-boiled and
finely grated
handful fresh flat-leaf parsley,
chopped, to serve

HOW TO DO IT

1 Heat 50g of the butter and 15ml (1 tbsp) of the honey in a frying pan over medium heat. Add the garlic and breadcrumbs and fry, stirring continuously, until the breadcrumbs are brown and crisp.

2 Steam the asparagus until tender, drain and refresh in cold water.

3 Place the asparagus on a serving dish and scatter with the breadcrumb mixture, eggs and parsley. Serve drizzled with the remaining melted butter and honey.

Wild mushrooms with tarragon, pearl barley and lemon crème fraîche

RECIPE BY **ROBYN TIMSON** FOR **VICKI CLARKE** AND **NIKKI GASKELL** PHOTOGRAPH BY **GRAEME WYLLIE**

Serves 4 **EASY** 40 mins

THE FLAVOUR COMBINATIONS
zest and juice of 2 lemons
250g crème fraîche
salt and freshly ground black
pepper, to taste
30ml (2 tbsp) olive oil
50g butter
500g (2 punnets) mixed wild
mushrooms, cut into chunks
handful fresh tarragon, chopped
200g (1 cup) pearl barley, cooked
according to packet instructions

HOW TO DO IT

1 For the lemon crème fraîche, fold the zest into the crème fraîche and season to taste.

2 Heat the oil in a pan. When it is just about at smoking point, add the butter and mushrooms and cook until the mushrooms are just brown and soft. Stir in the tarragon, lemon juice and barley.

3 Season and serve immediately with the lemon crème fraîche.

Tabbouleh with roasted cumin tomatoes, aubergines, cucumber and mint

RECIPE BY **KAREN SHORT** STYLING BY **HELENA ERASMUS** PHOTOGRAPH BY **GRAEME BORCHERS**

Serves 4 **EASY** 1 hr

THE FLAVOUR COMBINATIONS
TABBOULEH
250g bulgur wheat
500ml (2 cups) hot water
2 spring onions, chopped
50ml fresh mint and chives, chopped
zest and juice of 2 lemons
1 cucumber, diced into 2cm cubes
salt and freshly ground black pepper, to taste

ROASTED CUMIN TOMATOES
400g cocktail tomatoes, halved
10ml (2 tsp) cumin seeds, ground
30ml (2 tbsp) olive oil
50ml balsamic vinegar
4 sprigs fresh thyme
20ml (4 tsp) brown sugar

AUBERGINES
2 medium-sized aubergines, cubed
80ml (⅓ cup) olive oil
20ml (4 tsp) ground coriander
2 sprigs fresh rosemary
4 garlic cloves, peeled

HOW TO DO IT

1 Preheat the oven to 180°C. Place the bulgur wheat in a large bowl and pour the hot water over. Stir, cover with cling film and set aside to rest until the water is absorbed and the bulgur wheat is tender, about 15 minutes. Drain the excess water through a strainer. Transfer the bulgur wheat to a bowl and add the spring onions, herbs, zest, juice and cucumber. Season and set aside.

2 For the tomatoes, place them on a baking tray and sprinkle with the cumin, 30ml (2 tbsp) olive oil, balsamic vinegar, thyme and sugar. Season to taste and roast the tomatoes until caramelised, about 15 minutes.

3 For the aubergines, place them in a roasting pan, drizzle with the 80ml (⅓ cup) olive oil and add the coriander, rosemary and garlic. Season to taste and roast, about 20 minutes. Set aside to cool.

4 Add the tomatoes and aubergines to the bulgur wheat and mix lightly. Adjust the seasoning and serve.

This salad is filling and nutritious and, with its refreshing hints of mint, perfect to cool down with on a warm evening.

Bacon-wrapped roast pears stuffed with cambozola, walnuts and chives

RECIPE BY **ANNA MONTALI** PHOTOGRAPH BY **VANESSA LEWIS**

Serves 4 **EASY** 10 mins

THE FLAVOUR COMBINATIONS
4 pears, cored and cut in half lengthways

FILLING
160g cambozola cheese
100g walnuts, chopped
50ml honey
45ml (3 tbsp) fresh chives, nipped
salt and freshly ground black pepper, to taste
4 bacon strips, sliced lengthways

rocket, watercress and baby spinach, to serve

HOW TO DO IT

1 Preheat the oven to 180°C. Place the pears on a baking tray and bake until they are just soft, about 5 minutes.

2 Mix the filling ingredients together, except the bacon, until well combined. Spoon into the hollows where the pear cores have been carved out. Wrap a slice of bacon around each pear half and return to the oven until the bacon is crispy.

3 Serve the pears on a bed of rocket, watercress and baby spinach.

Crispy herbed chicken with grilled lemon

RECIPE BY **ANNA MONTALI** PHOTOGRAPH BY **VANESSA LEWIS**

Serves 4 **EASY** 1 hr

THE FLAVOUR COMBINATIONS
1,2kg deboned chicken
salt and freshly ground black pepper
100ml olive oil
50ml fresh flat-leaf parsley, chopped
50ml fresh oregano, chopped
50ml fresh mint, chopped
50ml fresh thyme, chopped
4 garlic cloves, peeled and
finely chopped
1 lemon, sliced

green salad, to serve (optional)

HOW TO DO IT

1 Preheat the oven to 200°C. Pierce the skin of the deboned chicken with a knife to prevent it from curling up during cooking. Season well with salt and pepper to taste.

2 Mix the olive oil with the parsley, oregano, mint, thyme and garlic. Using your hands, rub the herb mixture all over the chicken and set aside to rest, 20 minutes.

3 Heat a griddle pan to hot, place the sliced lemon in the pan and grill the chicken skin-side down until crispy. Turn over and cook for a further 5 minutes. Wrap the handle of the pan with foil and place in the oven, about 10 minutes. Allow to rest for 5 minutes before carving.

4 Serve the chicken with the grilled lemon and a green salad, if desired.

Lamb chops with grilled aubergines and minty mushy peas

RECIPE BY **LEILA SAFFARIAN** ASSISTED BY **NOMVUSULELO MNCUBE** PHOTOGRAPH BY **DYLAN SWART**

Serves 4 **EASY** 30 mins

THE FLAVOUR COMBINATIONS
8 lamb chops
30ml (2 tbsp) olive oil
squeeze lemon juice
salt and freshly ground black
pepper, to taste
1 aubergine, thinly sliced
400g frozen peas, blanched
45ml (3 tbsp) fresh mint, chopped +
extra, to serve

HOW TO DO IT

1 Season the chops with 15ml (1 tbsp) of the olive oil, the lemon juice and salt and pepper. Heat a large griddle pan and grill the chops to your liking. Remove from the heat and set aside.

2 Brush the aubergine with the remaining olive oil and grill on a griddle pan, 2 minutes on each side.

3 Place the peas, mint and seasoning in a bowl and use a hand blender to blitz the peas to form a chunky purée.

4 Serve the lamb chops with the griddled aubergine slices and minty peas. Garnish with mint leaves.

The freshness of the minted peas balances
the richness of the lamb perfectly.

258

Asian blackened ribs

RECIPE BY **JULES MERCER** STYLING BY **TARA SLOGGETT** PHOTOGRAPH BY **TOBY MURPHY**

Serves 6 (as a snack) **EASY** 2 hrs

THE FLAVOUR COMBINATIONS
1kg pork ribs, cut into
individual slices
oil, to fry
1 small onion, peeled and
finely chopped
3 garlic cloves, peeled and sliced
1 stick ginger (about a finger length),
peeled and grated
100g sticky dark brown sugar
45ml (3 tbsp) sherry/Chinese
Shaoxing wine
80ml ($^1/_3$ cup) Chinese black/
balsamic vinegar
80ml ($^1/_3$ cup) soya sauce

HOW TO DO IT

1 Place the ribs in a large pot with enough water to cover and bring to a boil, 15 – 20 minutes.

2 In a large saucepan over medium heat, heat a glug of oil and fry the onion and garlic until soft. Add the ginger and stir in the brown sugar, sherry or wine, vinegar and soya sauce. Turn off the heat until the ribs are cooked.

3 Once the ribs are ready, remove and drain, reserving 250ml (1 cup) cooking liquid. Add the ribs and cooking liquid to the sticky sauce, cover and cook over low heat until the sauce is sticky and dark brown, about 1 hour.

4 Remove the ribs and place on a serving platter. Leave the remaining sauce in the pot, turn the heat to high and boil until the sauce has thickened and is rich and glossy, 5 – 10 minutes. Drizzle over the ribs and serve warm.

dairy FREE

261

Honey-and-lemon semifreddo

RECIPE BY **LEILA SAFFARIAN** PHOTOGRAPH BY **GRAEME WYLLIE**

Serves 6 – 8 **EASY** 4 hrs

THE FLAVOUR COMBINATIONS
1 large egg
4 large egg yolks
**125ml (½ cup) honey + extra,
to drizzle**
310ml (1¼ cups) fresh cream
zest of 1 lemon + extra, to garnish
squeeze lemon juice

HOW TO DO IT

1 In a large heatproof bowl, beat the egg and egg yolks with the honey over a saucepan of simmering water (do not allow the bowl to touch the water) until the mixture is thick and pale.

2 Whip the cream until thick and gently fold into the egg-and-honey mixture.

3 Add the lemon zest and juice and fold in. Pour into a loaf tin and drizzle with extra honey. Cover with cling film and freeze, 3 – 4 hours.

4 When ready to serve, turn out the semifreddo onto a serving plate, drizzle with extra honey and garnish with lemon zest before slicing.

Baklava ice cream served with a cinnamon- and star anise-infused fruit compote

RECIPE BY **KAREN SHORT** STYLING BY **HELENA ERASMUS** PHOTOGRAPH BY **GRAEME BORCHERS**

Serves 6 **EASY** 1 hr 15 mins

THE FLAVOUR COMBINATIONS
50ml ground almonds
50ml pistachios, finely chopped
80ml (⅓ cup) ground cinnamon
10ml (2 tsp) castor sugar
4 sheets filo pastry
40g butter, melted
1L (4 cups) good-quality
vanilla ice cream

SYRUP
75g castor sugar
80ml (⅓ cup) water
juice of ½ lemon

COMPOTE
350ml orange juice
500ml (2 cups) red wine
200ml old brown sherry
320g sugar
2 cinnamon sticks
4 star anise
400g mixed dried fruit (we used
apricot, mango, figs and raisins,
but you can use any fruit)

fresh mint, to garnish

HOW TO DO IT

1 Preheat the oven to 180°C. Mix the almonds, pistachios, cinnamon and 10ml (2 tsp) castor sugar together in a bowl and set aside.

2 Brush all the pastry sheets with the melted butter and place them one on top of the other. Cut 24 rounds of pastry with a sharp knife to fit 6cm dariole moulds. Place the circles of pastry on a baking tray and sprinkle with the nut mixture. Bake until golden brown, about 5 minutes. Remove from oven and allow to cool completely.

3 For the syrup, add the 75g castor sugar, water and lemon juice to a saucepan and boil gently for a few minutes until syrupy. Leave to cool.

4 Line 6 dariole moulds with cling film, place one of the baked filo stacks in the bottom of the mould and drizzle with the sugar syrup. Soften the ice cream and press down on top of the filo disc. Repeat the process until the moulds are full. Place the last circle on top of the ice cream and pour the remaining syrup over. Transfer to the freezer.

5 For the compote, place the orange juice, wine, sherry, 320g sugar, cinnamon sticks and star anise in a large saucepan over medium heat and cook, stirring continuously, until the sugar has dissolved. Simmer for about 5 minutes before adding the dried fruit. Bring to a boil, lower the heat and simmer gently until the fruit is tender, 30 – 40 minutes. Allow to cool, then taste. Store the compote in its syrup in the fridge until ready to serve.

6 Remove the darioles from the freezer 10 minutes before serving to allow the ice cream to soften. Remove from the moulds and serve on a platter topped with the dried-fruit compote and fresh mint.

Cinnamon and star anise add an air of extravagance to a simple ice-cream dessert.

265

Dark-chocolate brownie cake

RECIPE BY **NICKY GIBBS** PHOTOGRAPH BY **ROELENE PRINSLOO**

Makes 1 **EASY** 1 hr

THE FLAVOUR COMBINATIONS
360g butter
100g dark chocolate, chopped
150g cocoa powder
6 large eggs, separated
360g castor sugar
240g cake flour
15ml (1 tbsp) baking powder
100ml milk

ICING
80g butter, softened
60g icing sugar
40g cocoa powder
30ml (2 tbsp) milk
30ml (2 tbsp) golden syrup

wafers, to decorate

HOW TO DO IT

1 Preheat the oven to 180°C, and butter and flour two 22cm springform cake tins.

2 Melt the 360g butter in a small saucepan over low heat. Add the chocolate and 150g cocoa powder and stir until well combined. Remove from the heat.

3 Whisk the egg whites in a bowl to stiff peaks.

4 In a separate bowl, whisk the egg yolks and castor sugar together until light and fluffy.

5 Slowly add the chocolate mixture to the yolk mixture and whisk until well combined.

6 Sift the flour and baking powder into the mixture and beat well. Add the 100ml milk and mix until smooth.

7 Carefully fold the egg whites into the chocolate batter.

8 Divide the batter between the cake tins and bake until a skewer inserted into the centre of the cakes comes out clean, 25 – 30 minutes.

9 Remove the cakes from the oven and allow to cool on a wire rack before icing.

10 For the icing, beat the 80g butter and icing sugar together until light and fluffy. Whisk in the 40g cocoa a little at a time until incorporated. Add the 30ml (2 tbsp) milk and syrup and whisk until smooth.

11 Spread some of the icing evenly all over one of the cooled cakes and sandwich it together with the other cake. Spread the remaining icing to cover both cakes and decorate with wafers to serve.

COOK'S TIPS
You can sandwich the two halves of this cake together with cream, jam or a combination of raspberries and cream. If you like, top the cake with nuts or add nuts to the batter.

THE MONTH OF November

IT'S ALMOST THE END OF THE YEAR, BUT NOT QUITE... KEEP EVERYONE IN GOOD SPIRITS IN THE LEAD UP TO THE FESTIVE SEASON WITH OUR DELICIOUS SELECTION OF EATS THIS MONTH – SUMMERY, FRESH AND SO GOOD, YOU WON'T WANT IT TO END

Home-made lemon-and-ginger tonic

RECIPE AND STYLING BY **JACQUES ERASMUS** PHOTOGRAPH BY **MICKY HOYLE**

Serves 6 **EASY** 10 mins

THE FLAVOUR COMBINATIONS
200ml lemon juice
120g sugar
5cm fresh ginger, peeled and minced
pinch salt
500ml (2 cups) crushed ice
1L (4 cups) tonic water

lemon leaves, to garnish
sliced lemons, to serve

HOW TO DO IT

1 Combine the lemon juice, sugar, ginger and salt, and mix well.

2 Add the crushed ice and top with tonic water.

3 Garnish with lemon leaves and serve with sliced lemons.

Mandazi bread

RECIPE BY **ABBI BEN YEHUDIN** AND **GIZELLE KENNEL** PHOTOGRAPH BY **RUSSELL SMITH**

Serves 30 **EASY** 30 mins + proving time

THE FLAVOUR COMBINATIONS
800g cake flour + extra, to dust
10g instant dry yeast
15ml (1 tbsp) sugar
25ml (5 tsp) cumin seeds, roasted
25ml (5 tsp) caraway seeds, roasted
10ml (2 tsp) salt
280ml hot (not boiling) water
60ml (¼ cup) olive oil
750ml (3 cups) sunflower oil

HOW TO DO IT
1 Combine the flour, yeast, sugar, seeds and salt in a bowl.
2 Add the water and olive oil and mix together to form a sticky dough.
3 Knead the dough for 10 minutes on a floured surface. Return to the bowl and cover with cling film. Leave in a warm place until the dough has doubled in size.
4 Roll out a 30cm square (about 1cm thick) of dough on a floured surface. Cut into long strips. Place in boiling-hot sunflower oil until puffed up and golden. Serve immediately.

This warm and spicy bread is delicious with any drink and makes a welcome change from cheese straws.

No-set chicken, apricot and cucumber terrine

RECIPE AND STYLING BY **ILLANIQUE VAN ASWEGEN** PHOTOGRAPH BY **ADEL FERREIRA**

Serves 4 **EASY** 30 mins

THE FLAVOUR COMBINATIONS
320g chicken breasts, cooked
5 dried apricots, finely chopped
15ml (1 tbsp) fresh chives,
finely chopped
15ml (1 tbsp) spring onion,
thinly sliced
3 piquanté peppers, finely chopped
180g plain cream cheese,
at room temperature
salt and freshly ground black
pepper, to taste
pinch ground paprika
pinch dried chilli flakes (optional)
2 cucumbers

sprouts, to garnish
grilled bread, to serve

HOW TO DO IT

1 Shred the chicken into bite-sized pieces. Combine with the chopped apricots, chives, spring onion and piquanté peppers. Gently fold in the cream cheese. Season to taste and add the paprika and chilli flakes, if desired.

2 Use a vegetable peeler to peel 12 long ribbons from the cucumbers. Slightly overlap 6 ribbons on a clean surface to form a 'sheet'. Place half of the filling on one side of the sheet and roll up tightly to form a cylinder. Repeat with the remaining filling and cucumber ribbons.

3 Gently cut the terrine into rounds, top with sprouts and serve on the bread.

Radicchio and butter lettuce salad with mozzarella fritters, radishes and anchovy dressing

RECIPE AND STYLING BY **VICKI CLARKE** AND **NIKKI GASKELL** PHOTOGRAPH BY **ELSA YOUNG**

Serves 4 **EASY** 20 mins

THE FLAVOUR COMBINATIONS
2-day-old herbed naan bread
small handful fresh flat-leaf parsley,
basil and mint, roughly chopped
salt and freshly ground black
pepper, to taste
sunflower oil, to fry
4 buffalo mozzarella balls,
each torn into 4 pieces
cake flour, to dust
1 large egg, beaten
1 head butter lettuce,
leaves separated
100g radicchio leaves
6 radishes, thinly sliced
24 Kalamata olives

ANCHOVY DRESSING
60ml (¼ cup) raspberry vinegar
125ml (½ cup) sunflower oil
6 anchovy fillets, very thinly sliced
5ml (1 tsp) Dijon mustard

watercress, to garnish

HOW TO DO IT
1 In a blender, process the naan to rough crumbs. Transfer to a bowl, add the herbs and season to taste.

2 In a shallow pan, heat the sunflower oil. Dust the mozzarella pieces in the flour and shake off any excess. Dip the mozzarella in the egg and then into the naan mixture. Pat well to press in the crumbs.

3 Drop the balls into the heated oil and fry until golden brown, 1 – 2 minutes. Drain on paper towel and set aside.

4 For the dressing, combine all of the ingredients in a cup and whisk well.

5 Divide the salad leaves, radishes and olives among 4 bowls. Top with the warm mozzarella balls, drizzle with the dressing and garnish with fresh watercress.

276

Peanut-and-vegetable parcels

RECIPE AND STYLING BY **LEILA SAFFARIAN** PHOTOGRAPH BY **DYLAN SWART**

Serves 6 – 8 **EASY** 45 mins

THE FLAVOUR COMBINATIONS
30ml (2 tbsp) olive oil
1 small onion, peeled and diced
kernels of 1 corn on the cob
2 carrots, peeled and grated
4 baby marrows, diced
5ml (1 tsp) ground coriander
5ml (1 tsp) ground cumin
2,5ml (½ tsp) turmeric
2,5ml (½ tsp) ground cardamom
1 red chilli, seeded and finely chopped
Maldon Sea Salt and freshly ground black pepper, to taste
100g unsalted peanuts + extra, to serve
8 sheets filo pastry
100g butter, melted
2 red peppers, roasted + extra, to serve

lime wedges, to serve
julienned spring onions, to serve

HOW TO DO IT

1 Preheat the oven to 180°C. Heat the oil in a large non-stick frying pan over medium heat, add the onion and fry until golden. Add the corn, carrots and baby marrows and fry for 2 minutes.

2 Add the spices and season well to taste. Fry for a further 5 minutes, add the peanuts and set aside to cool.

3 When the mixture has cooled, cut the filo pastry sheets into 4 squares, brush with melted butter and add 10ml (2 tsp) mixture to each.

4 Gather the pastry edges together and gently twist to enclose the filling. Place on a baking tray lined with baking paper, brush with the remaining butter and bake in the preheated oven until golden, about 10 minutes.

5 For the red-pepper sauce, place the peppers in a blender and blitz to form a smooth paste.

6 Serve the peanut-and-vegetable parcels with the red-pepper sauce, lime wedges, spring onions, extra peanuts and roasted peppers on the side.

These spicy bites incorporate earthy flavours in a crisp parcel. Using filo pastry makes them lighter, crunchier and healthier, and the roasted-pepper sauce adds a smoky flavour.

Yellowtail-and-tomato kebabs served in a cardamom butter sauce

RECIPE AND STYLING BY **ANNA MONTALI** PHOTOGRAPH BY **VANESSA GROBLER**

Serves 4 **EASY** 2 hrs 20 mins

THE FLAVOUR COMBINATIONS
20 yellowtail cubes
4 large tomatoes, quartered

MARINADE
60ml (¼ cup) olive oil
20ml (4 tsp) fresh flat-leaf parsley, finely chopped
20ml (4 tsp) fresh lemon juice
10ml (2 tsp) smoked paprika
salt and freshly ground black pepper, to taste
1 garlic clove, peeled and finely chopped

SAUCE
50ml good-quality chicken stock
seeds of 5 cardamom pods
juice of 1 lime
20ml (4 tsp) dry sherry
20g butter

HOW TO DO IT

1 Thread the fish cubes and tomatoes, alternating, onto long stainless-steel skewers and place in an oval dish.

2 Mix all of the marinade ingredients together, pour over the kebabs and refrigerate to marinate, 2 hours.

3 Braai, turning continuously until done, about 20 minutes.

4 For the sauce, heat the stock over low heat, add the cardamom seeds, lime juice and sherry, and stir to combine. Cook until the mixture has thickened a little, about 10 minutes. Remove from heat and stir in the butter.

5 To serve, place the kebabs on a platter and pour the sauce over.

*I left the skin on to prevent the fish from breaking up,
but this is a matter of personal choice.*

A fantastic way to start any summer meal. It has texture, flavour and overall good looks. You can replace the papaya with watermelon when in season.

Crispy duck with cucumber, papaya and sweet miso

RECIPE BY **CHEYNE MORRISBY** PHOTOGRAPH BY **SEAN CALITZ**

Serves 4 **EASY** 45 mins

THE FLAVOUR COMBINATIONS
2 duck breasts
45ml (3 tbsp) miso paste
150ml mirin (sweet Japanese cooking wine)
1 cucumber
1 medium-sized papaya, sliced
15ml (1 tbsp) coriander seeds
15ml (1 tbsp) black sesame seeds
150g cashews, crushed

cherry tomatoes, sliced, to garnish
fresh coriander, to garnish

HOW TO DO IT

1 Preheat the oven to 180°C. In a hot, non-stick frying pan, pan-fry the duck breasts, skin-side down, until crisp. Remove from pan and place in the oven for 10 minutes. Remove from oven (leave the oven on) and slice each duck breast into small strips.

2 Mix the miso and the mirin into a soft paste. Brush the sliced duck all over with 30ml (2 tbsp) miso mixture. Return the duck to the hot oven and roast until crisp and golden, about 20 minutes. Remove from oven and allow to cool for a few minutes.

3 Peel the cucumber and use a vegetable peeler to shave off long slices that look like thick noodles.

4 Arrange the cucumber noodles in the centre of a plate. Arrange slices of papaya around the cucumber. Sprinkle the coriander seeds and black sesame seeds over the papaya. Arrange slices of duck on the plate. Spoon over the rest of the miso mixture and sprinkle with the cashews. Serve garnished with cherry tomatoes and coriander.

Fillet medallion with haloumi and summer salsa

RECIPE AND STYLING BY **LOUISE THOMAS** AND **CLIVE JOHNSON** PHOTOGRAPH BY **FRANCOIS BOOYENS**

Serves 4 **EASY** 30 mins + 2 hrs, to marinate

THE FLAVOUR COMBINATIONS
MARINADE
125ml (½ cup) soya sauce
125ml (½ cup) sweet-chilli sauce
30ml (2 tbsp) honey
250ml (1 cup) oil
½ onion, peeled and finely chopped
2 garlic cloves, peeled and crushed
30ml (2 tbsp) coriander seeds
5 fresh basil leaves

4 x 200g beef fillet medallions

SALSA
150g thin green asparagus
1 red pepper, seeded and cubed
1 x 420g tin whole-kernel corn, rinsed and drained
45ml (3 tbsp) olive oil + extra, to drizzle
zest and juice of 1 lemon
30ml (2 tbsp) fresh flat-leaf parsley, chopped
20ml (4 tsp) red-wine vinegar
salt and cracked black pepper, to taste

250g haloumi cheese, cubed

HOW TO DO IT

1 Preheat the oven to 200°C. Mix all of the marinade ingredients together and pour over the fillet. Cover and refrigerate to marinate, at least 2 hours.

2 For the salsa, remove the woody ends of the asparagus and blanch in salted, boiling water until just cooked. Submerge in ice water, drain and slice.

3 Place the pepper and corn on a baking tray and drizzle with 30ml (2 tbsp) of the olive oil and the lemon juice. Scatter the lemon zest on top and roast in the oven until just cooked and softened. Remove from oven, but leave the oven on. Toss the asparagus, pepper mixture and parsley together with the vinegar and a drizzle of the oil. Season to taste.

4 Place each piece of fillet on a hot griddle pan and sear on both sides. Place on a baking tray and bake in the oven, 10 – 15 minutes. Remove from oven and rest for a few minutes.

5 Heat a pan with the remaining olive oil and fry the haloumi until golden.

6 To serve, top the fillet medallions with the haloumi and salsa.

A fun alternative
to the usual
F R I E D
DOUGHNUTS

Mini gooseberry and vanilla doughnuts with white-chocolate glaze

RECIPE AND STYLING BY **ILLANIQUE VAN ASWEGEN** PHOTOGRAPH BY **ADEL FERREIRA** ASSISTED BY **JÖMERI MOUTON**

Makes 12 mini doughnuts **EASY** 40 mins

THE FLAVOUR COMBINATIONS
DOUGHNUTS

150g sugar
150g cake flour
6,25ml (1¼ tsp) baking powder
1,25ml (¼ tsp) fine salt
125ml (½ cup) buttermilk
1 large egg
seeds of ½ vanilla pod
30g unsalted butter, melted
180g fresh gooseberries, halved

WHITE-CHOCOLATE GLAZE

150g white chocolate,
roughly chopped
130g icing sugar, sifted
30ml (2 tbsp) milk
seeds of ¼ vanilla pod/2,5ml (½ tsp)
vanilla paste

12 gooseberries, halved, to serve
fresh mint leaves, to garnish

HOW TO DO IT

1 Preheat the oven to 180°C. Lightly grease a mini doughnut pan. Sift the sugar, flour, baking powder and salt together in a mixing bowl. Whisk in the buttermilk, egg, seeds of ½ vanilla pod and melted butter until smooth. Stir in the 180g halved gooseberries.

2 Add a spoonful of the mixture to each doughnut hole in the tin, filling them about halfway only – the mixture rises quite a bit during baking. Make sure there are a few pieces of gooseberry in each one. Bake for 6 – 8 minutes. The doughnuts are cooked when a cake skewer inserted into the centre of a doughnut comes out clean. Allow to cool on a wire rack.

3 For the glaze, melt the chocolate in a double boiler over low heat, then allow to cool for a few minutes. Combine the icing sugar, milk, seeds of ¼ vanilla pod or 2,5ml (½ tsp) vanilla paste in a mixing bowl and stir until smooth. Add to the slightly cooled chocolate and whisk to combine.

4 Immediately dip the tops of the doughnuts in the glaze and place 2 gooseberry halves on each. Garnish with fresh mint to serve.

COOK'S TIP
Find mini doughnut tins at your nearest cake supplies store. They come in different sizes.

287

Chai-spiced milk-and-honey jellies

RECIPE BY **LYN WOODWARD** STYLING BY **NATALIE BELL** PHOTOGRAPH BY **GRAEME WYLLIE**

Serves 6 **EASY** 35 mins + 3 – 4 hrs, to set

THE FLAVOUR COMBINATIONS

800ml milk
10 black peppercorns
2 cinnamon sticks, broken
6 cardamom pods, crushed
1 star anise
small pinch salt
60ml (¼ cup) honey + extra,
if needed
6 gelatine leaves, soaked in 60ml
(¼ cup) cold water

HOW TO DO IT

1 Heat the milk in a saucepan. Add the spices and salt and bring to a boil. Turn off the heat and leave to infuse, 20 minutes. Strain, return the liquid to the pot and stir in the honey (add more honey if you prefer it sweeter).

2 In a separate saucepan, gently heat 125ml (½ cup) of the mixture, add the softened gelatine leaves and stir until dissolved. Add the remaining liquid and stir well.

3 Divide among 6 serving glasses and refrigerate to chill until just set, 3 – 4 hours.

Chocolate-and-nut filo cigars served with a spicy syrup

RECIPE AND STYLING BY **ANNA MONTALI** PHOTOGRAPH BY **GRAEME BORCHERS**

Serves 12 **EASY** 30 mins

THE FLAVOUR COMBINATIONS
SPICY SYRUP
250ml (1 cup) water
150g sugar
zest and juice of 2 limes
1 red chilli, seeded and
finely chopped
2 star anise pods

FILO CIGARS
200g good-quality dark chocolate,
broken into pieces
200g mixed nuts, coarsely chopped
5ml (1 tsp) ground cinnamon
5ml (1 tsp) ground cloves
200g filo pastry
50g butter, melted

HOW TO DO IT

1 Preheat the oven to 200°C. For the syrup, place the water and sugar in a saucepan over medium heat and stir until the sugar has melted. Add the remaining ingredients and cook until a syrupy consistency is achieved.

2 For the cigars, melt the chocolate in a double boiler. Add the nuts and spices and stir to combine.

3 Place the filo pastry on a work surface and cut out twenty-four 13cm x 9cm pieces. Brush one piece of filo with the butter. Top with another piece of filo. Pour about 30ml (2 tbsp) chocolate mixture on one end of the filo, fold the sides in to contain the mixture and roll to form a cigar. Repeat with the remaining filo pieces and chocolate mixture.

4 Bake the cigars until golden and crispy, about 10 minutes. Remove and place in the syrup for about 2 minutes. Just before serving, insert a bamboo skewer into each cigar.

Make sure these sweet morsels
are soaked in the syrup.

Raspberry ripple semifreddo

RECIPE BY **ANNA MONTALI** ASSISTED BY **NOMVUSELELO MNCUBE** STYLING BY **INGRID CASSON** PHOTOGRAPH BY **GRAEME BORCHERS**

Makes 10 **EASY** 1 hr +
overnight, to freeze

THE FLAVOUR COMBINATIONS
4 large eggs
2 large egg yolks
60ml (¼ cup) vanilla extract
210g castor sugar
500ml (2 cups) fresh cream
130g fresh or frozen raspberries

10 wafer cones, to serve
100g dark chocolate, melted, to serve

HOW TO DO IT

1 For the semifreddo, combine the eggs, yolks, vanilla and sugar in a heatproof glass bowl over a pot of simmering water and beat with an electric hand-held mixer until thick and pale, about 20 minutes. Do not allow the bottom of the bowl to touch the water.

2 Remove from the heat and place the bowl on a cloth so that it doesn't move around. Continue to beat until cool, about a further 20 minutes.

3 In a separate bowl, beat the cream to stiff peaks. Gently fold the cream into the egg mixture until well combined. Spoon the mixture into a 2L ice-cream container.

4 For the ripple, place half of the raspberries in a food processor and blend until smooth. Spoon the blended raspberries and the whole raspberries over the semifreddo, using a fork to create a ripple effect. Cover and freeze overnight.

5 To serve, gently lower each cone into the melted chocolate to coat the rims. Scoop a ball of semifreddo into each cone and hand out.

COOK'S TIPS
This is a semifreddo, not a full ice cream, which means it melts faster, so use immediately after removing from the freezer. Any seasonal fruit can be used instead of raspberries. Once the rims of the cones are coated in melted chocolate, you can also dip them into finely chopped nuts or desiccated coconut before adding to the semifreddo.

THE MONTH OF

December

IT'S FINALLY HERE! THE MOST WONDERFUL TIME OF THE YEAR. A TIME WHERE WE CAN OVERINDULGE WITHOUT FEELING GUILTY; A TIME TO DRINK THE FINEST WINES AND COCKTAILS, TO RELISH IN RICH, DELICIOUS AND TRADITIONAL DISHES THAT RING OF CHRISTMAS, LOVE AND CELEBRATION. WE'VE PUT TOGETHER A WOW-WORTHY FESTIVE FEAST (INCLUDING SOME TASTY CANAPÉS AND A BOOSTER WELCOME DRINK), AS WELL AS A SELECTION OF MEALS IN THE LEAD UP TO THE BIG DAY. PLUS, DON'T MISS OUR IDEAS FOR USING UP THOSE LEFTOVERS. MERRY CHRISTMAS AND ENJOY!

Sparkling wine with raspberry granita

RECIPE AND STYLING BY **KIM HOEPFL** PHOTOGRAPH BY **VANESSA GROBLER**

Serves 4 – 6 **EASY** 3 mins +
overnight, to refrigerate

THE FLAVOUR COMBINATIONS
500ml (2 cups) raspberry juice
750ml (3 cups) dry sparkling wine,
well chilled

HOW TO DO IT

1 Pour the raspberry juice in a bowl and refrigerate overnight until frozen.

2 To make the granita, scrape the frozen raspberry juice with a fork to create a mass of ice crystals.

3 Half fill Champagne flutes with the granita, top with sparkling wine and serve immediately.

This is an elegant welcome drink. It also makes
an attractive and refreshing dessert.

Honeyed nuts and fruit

RECIPE BY **INGRID CASSON** AND **LEILA SAFFARIAN** ASSISTED BY **ITUMELENG MASONDO** PHOTOGRAPH BY **GRAEME BORCHERS**

Makes 2 jars **EASY** 15 mins

THE FLAVOUR COMBINATIONS
150g cashew nuts
100g walnuts
100g Brazil nuts
500g honey
100g dried cranberries
2,5ml (½ tsp) ground ginger
1 cinnamon stick
2 strips orange peel

HOW TO DO IT

1 Place all of the ingredients in a large saucepan and slowly heat through over low heat.

2 When the honey is runny, remove from heat and spoon into sterilised jars.

3 Store at room temperature out of direct sunlight.

These sticky, honeyed nuts are great for serving with a selection of fruit and cheese or as an indulgent topping for plain sponge cakes or puddings.

This makes a super-stylish starter or canapé.
You can use salmon instead of tuna.

Tuna tartare with lime aïoli

RECIPE BY **KAREN SHORT** STYLING BY **HELENA ERASMUS** PHOTOGRAPH BY **GRAEME BORCHERS**

Serves 4 **EASY** 15 mins

THE FLAVOUR COMBINATIONS
TUNA TARTARE
250g fresh tuna, diced
pinch white pepper
20ml (4 tsp) olive oil
5ml (1 tsp) anchovies, finely chopped
10ml (2 tsp) fresh chives, chopped
10ml (2 tsp) soya sauce
10ml (2 tsp) mirin
5ml (1 tsp) salt
2,5ml (½ tsp) cayenne pepper
2,5ml (½ tsp) garlic, chopped
5ml (1 tsp) fresh ginger, peeled
and chopped
½ red onion, peeled and finely diced
salt and freshly ground black
pepper, to taste

LIME AÏOLI
250ml (1 cup) good-quality
mayonnaise
zest and juice of 2 limes
50ml fresh dill, chopped

sprouts, to garnish
lemon wedges, to serve

HOW TO DO IT

1 For the tartare, mix the tuna with the remaining tartare ingredients and season to taste.

2 For the lime aïoli, mix all of the ingredients together and season well to taste.

3 Divide the tuna among 4 plates or arrange on a platter. Serve topped with sprouts and with a side of the lime aïoli and lemon wedges for squeezing.

dairy FREE

COOK'S TIP
Tuna tartare can also be served with a crispy green salad and baguettes.

Aubergine, tomato and feta terrine topped with fresh basil

RECIPE BY **ILLANIQUE VAN ASWEGEN** PHOTOGRAPH BY **ADEL FERREIRA**

Serves 6 **EASY** 1 hr 30 mins

THE FLAVOUR COMBINATIONS
8 tomatoes, halved
15ml (1 tbsp) sugar
pinch salt
60g garlic butter
olive oil, to fry
3 large aubergines, thinly sliced lengthways
200g feta
125ml (½ cup) red-pepper pesto
salt and freshly ground black pepper, to taste

handful fresh basil, to garnish

HOW TO DO IT

1 Preheat the oven to 200°C. Place the tomatoes on a baking tray and lightly sprinkle with the sugar and salt. Roast in the oven until tender, but still holding their shape, 30 minutes.

2 Melt some of the garlic butter with a generous splash of oil and fry the aubergine slices in batches, a few at a time. Add more butter and oil as the aubergine absorbs it during cooking.

3 Pack the tomatoes, cut side down, into a 20cm ring tin, overlapping them to form a dense top layer.

4 Crumble the feta over the top of the tomatoes and pat down lightly with your hands to form the second layer. Lightly spread the pesto over and add the aubergines to form the final layer.

5 Once all of the layers are in the tin, cover with cling film and pat down one last time. Refrigerate to set for about 30 minutes.

6 Gently unmould onto a serving platter, season to taste and scatter fresh basil leaves on top to garnish.

302

Start your Christmas lunch with a delicious cold soup of strawberries, pear and sherry served with a dollop of crème fraîche.

Chilled strawberry-and-sherry soup

RECIPE BY **ANNA MONTALI** PHOTOGRAPH BY **ELSA YOUNG**

Serves 6 – 8 **EASY** 30 mins +
4 hrs, to chill

THE FLAVOUR COMBINATIONS
500ml (2 cups) water
100ml dry sherry
50ml sugar
juice of 2 lemons
1 cinnamon stick
500ml (2 cups) fresh strawberries,
puréed
1 pear, peeled, cored and puréed
30ml (2 tbsp) fresh coriander,
finely chopped
40ml crème fraîche
freshly ground black pepper, to taste

HOW TO DO IT

1 Mix together the water, sherry, sugar and lemon juice until the sugar has dissolved. Add the cinnamon stick and cook over medium heat, stirring occasionally, about 20 minutes.

2 Add the puréed strawberries and pear and continue to cook for 10 minutes. Discard the cinnamon and add the coriander. Stir to combine and refrigerate to chill, 4 hours.

3 Serve with a dollop of crème fraîche and season to taste with freshly ground black pepper.

COOK'S TIP
This dish can be made in advance. Add the crème fraîche and pepper just before serving.

Artichoke, asparagus and ricotta salad with red-onion dressing

RECIPE BY **ILLANIQUE VAN ASWEGEN** PHOTOGRAPH BY **ADEL FERREIRA**

Serves 2 **EASY** 1 hr

THE FLAVOUR COMBINATIONS
RED-ONION DRESSING
¼ red onion, peeled and thinly sliced
45ml (3 tbsp) red wine vinegar
30ml (2 tbsp) olive oil
2,5ml (½ tsp) Dijon mustard
pinch sugar

SALAD
3 whole artichokes
1 lemon
100g asparagus, blanched
½ spring onion, thinly sliced
handful mixed baby leaves/microherbs
60ml (¼ cup) ricotta

grilled bruschetta, to serve

HOW TO DO IT

1 For the dressing, place all of the ingredients in a clean jar and shake well to combine. Refrigerate while you prepare the salad.

2 For the salad, begin by preparing your artichokes. Bring a large pot of salted water to a boil and add a generous squeeze of lemon juice. Trim the stems of the artichokes, place them in boiling water and cook, 20 – 30 minutes, depending on their size. They are ready when the outer leaves come away easily when pulled.

3 Remove the outer leaves until you come to the central cone of soft, pale-yellow leaves. Cut off the tips if tough. Trim the bases to remove any hard bits. Halve the artichokes and scoop out the fuzzy, inner chokes from both halves. Rinse and squeeze over some lemon juice to prevent them from browning.

4 Thinly slice the artichoke hearts and combine with the soft, yellow artichoke leaves, asparagus and spring onion. Add the dressing and toss to combine.

5 Add the baby leaves or microherbs and crumble the ricotta over the salad just before serving. Serve with grilled bruschetta on the side.

306

Deep-fried artichokes with a jalapeño-and-bacon dip

RECIPE BY **ILLANIQUE VAN ASWEGEN** PHOTOGRAPH BY **ADEL FERREIRA**

Serves 2 – 4 **EASY** 1 hr

THE FLAVOUR COMBINATIONS
4 large whole artichokes
60ml (¼ cup) cake flour, seasoned
with salt and freshly ground
black pepper
3 large eggs, beaten
80ml (¹/₃ cup) breadcrumbs
30ml (2 tbsp) Parmesan,
finely grated
vegetable oil, to deep-fry

JALAPEÑO-AND-BACON DIP
150g bacon, diced
5ml (1 tsp) garlic, crushed
80g (2 large) gherkins,
finely chopped
1 pickled jalapeño pepper, seeded
and finely chopped
30ml (2 tbsp) spring onion,
finely chopped
150g Greek yoghurt
45ml (3 tbsp) cream cheese,
at room temperature
45ml (3 tbsp) mayonnaise
15ml (1 tbsp) sweet-chilli sauce
1,25ml (¼ tsp) paprika
5 fresh basil leaves, finely chopped

salt flakes, to serve
microherbs, to garnish (optional)
lemon wedges, to serve

HOW TO DO IT

1 Follow the steps in the previous recipe on how to cook the artichokes. You will have 8 halves.

2 Pat each half dry and dip into the seasoned flour. Dip into the eggs and then into a mixture of the breadcrumbs and Parmesan. Repeat with the remaining artichokes.

3 Heat enough vegetable oil in a pot to deep-fry the artichokes. When the oil is hot, gently drop the crumbed artichokes in and fry until golden and crisp, 1 – 2 minutes. Drain on paper towel.

4 For the dip, pan-fry the bacon over medium heat until crisp and golden. Add the crushed garlic halfway through the cooking process. Combine the cooked bacon with the chopped gherkins, jalapeño and spring onion, and set aside.

5 Blend the yoghurt, cream cheese, mayonnaise, sweet-chilli sauce and paprika together until smooth. Add this to the bacon mixture and season to taste. Stir in the fresh basil and refrigerate until ready to serve.

6 Serve the artichokes sprinkled with salt and garnished with microherbs, if desired. Add a side of the dipping sauce and some lemon wedges for squeezing.

Magical mince pies

RECIPE BY **VICKI CLARKE** AND **NIKKI WEFELMEIER** PHOTOGRAPH BY **ELSA YOUNG**

Serves 24 **EASY** 45 mins

THE FLAVOUR COMBINATIONS
cake flour, to dust
400g shortcrust pastry
1 x 454g jar fruit mincemeat
20ml (4 tsp) milk, to brush
icing sugar, to dust

HOW TO DO IT

1 Preheat the oven to 180°C. Lightly grease two standard (12-well) muffin trays.

2 On a dusted working surface, roll out the pastry and cut out rounds to fit the bottom and sides of the muffin wells.

3 Fill three quarters of each pastry cup with mincemeat. Roll out the remaining pastry and cut out shapes, such as stars or hearts. Dampen the edges slightly with a little water and place the shapes on top of the mincemeat. Brush with a little milk to give the pies a matte finish.

4 Bake until golden, about 20 minutes. Cool on a wire rack, dust with icing sugar and serve.

COOK'S TIPS
For a glossier finish, brush each pie with a beaten egg instead of milk. You can store these pies in an airtight container, or freeze them for up to 1 month.

These pies are much easier to make than you think and so much tastier than store-bought ones. Serve them in your favourite silver bowl.

Christmas turkey

RECIPE BY **RUDI LIEBENBERG** PHOTOGRAPH BY **VANESSA GROBLER**

Serves 10 – 12 **EASY** ± 5 hrs

**THE FLAVOUR COMBINATIONS
STUFFING (ENOUGH FOR
A 7KG TURKEY)**
700g white bread, diced
15ml (1 tbsp) olive oil
2 medium onions, peeled and diced
100g bacon, coarsely minced
(optional)
50g chicken livers, minced (optional)
2 celery sticks, diced
4 garlic cloves, peeled and
finely chopped
45g butter
3 Granny Smith apples, diced
15ml (1 tbsp) sugar
125ml (½ cup) pecan nuts,
roughly chopped
30ml (2 tbsp) fresh sage, chopped
30ml (2 tbsp) fresh thyme, chopped
125ml (½ cup) apple cider
125ml (½ cup) chicken stock
salt and freshly ground black
pepper, to taste

TURKEY
7kg turkey
100g butter, softened
10ml (2 tsp) fresh flat-leaf parsley
10ml (2 tsp) fresh sage, chopped
2 garlic cloves, peeled and crushed
20ml (4 tsp) salt
10ml (2 tsp) freshly ground
black pepper
500ml (2 cups) chicken stock
30g butter, melted

MIREPOIX
200g carrots, cubed
2 leeks, cubed
1 celery stick, cubed
1 onion, peeled and cubed

**SAUCE (MADE USING THE
RESERVED PAN JUICES)**
100ml – 150ml white wine/apple
cider/sherry
beurre manié, as required (a dough
consisting of equal parts soft butter
and flour, used to thicken sauces
and soups)
50g chicken/turkey livers, minced
10ml (2 tsp) fresh thyme sprigs
10ml (2 tsp) fresh sage
2 fresh bay leaves
100ml fresh cream (optional)

HOW TO DO IT

1 A day before preparing the turkey, make the stuffing by placing the bread on a baking tray and drying it in a low-heat oven for about 45 minutes.

2 In a large frying pan, heat the olive oil and sauté the onion until translucent. Add the bacon, chicken livers, celery and garlic. Add the butter, apples and sugar and allow to caramelise, 5 – 8 minutes. Stir in the nuts, herbs, apple cider and stock. Scrape the sediment loose and cook until reduced by half. Season to taste.

3 Add the bread and allow all of the liquid to be absorbed. Cook until the stuffing is soft, 5 – 6 minutes.

4 Preheat the oven to 160°C. Remove the turkey from the fridge at least 1 hour before roasting. The stuffing can be heated slightly before use.

5 For the turkey, loosen the skin from the bird and stuff with the softened butter, herbs and garlic. Stuff the turkey cavity loosely (the stuffing will expand). Close the cavity and truss the turkey by tying the legs together.

6 Rub the salt and pepper all over the turkey. Pour a little of the chicken stock into a roasting pan and top with the turkey and mirepoix ingredients. Brush the turkey with the melted butter.

7 Place a piece of foil over the top of the turkey and roast for 1 hour, making sure there is enough stock at the base of the turkey. Baste the turkey with more butter. Continue roasting and check again after 2 hours. Baste again after 3 hours, remove the foil, baste and continue roasting for a further 30 minutes.

8 Remove the turkey and set aside to rest. Reserve all of the pan juices for the sauce.

9 For the sauce, bring the reserved juices to a boil and add the wine, apple cider or sherry. Thicken with the beurre manié, making sure it is cooked out and thoroughly combined. Add the livers, herbs and cream, if desired. Strain the sauce.

10 Serve the turkey with the sauce and your favourite accompaniments, such as fondant potatoes, chipolata sausages wrapped in bacon, and dried apricots wrapped in bay leaves.

313

Naartjie and ginger beer-glazed gammon

RECIPE, STYLING AND PHOTOGRAPH BY **KATELYN WILLIAMS**

Serves 12 **EASY** 4 hrs

THE FLAVOUR COMBINATIONS
2kg – 3kg cured and smoked
gammon, bone left in
2L (8 cups) ginger beer
rind and juice of 5 naartjies
1 onion, peeled and halved
3 star anise
1 cinnamon stick
45ml (3 tbsp) muscovado sugar
handful cloves

HOW TO DO IT

1 Preheat the oven to 150°C. Place the gammon, skin-side down, in a large ovenproof roasting dish. Pour over 1,5L (6 cups) of the ginger beer, add the naartjie rind and juice from 3 of the naartjies, the onion, star anise and cinnamon stick. Cover the roasting dish with foil and place in the oven until the ham is tender, about 3 hours and 30 minutes. Pour off the cooking liquid and allow to cool slightly. Leave the oven on.

2 In a small saucepan over low heat, warm the remaining ginger beer, naartjie rind and juice, and the sugar until dissolved. Bring to a boil, then simmer until slightly thickened to form a glaze, about 5 minutes. Increase the oven temperature to 200°C.

3 Lift the skin off the gammon, leaving a layer of fat, then score the fat into diamond shapes. Press a clove into the tips of each diamond shape, then return the gammon to the ovenproof dish. Brush with the glaze and roast in the oven until caramelised, basting every now and then until golden brown and glossy, 20 – 30 minutes.

COOK'S TIP
Caramelise naartjie slices in a pan with a little muscovado sugar and serve with the gammon for a South African take on the traditional pineapple slices.

Karoo steamed Christmas pudding

RECIPE BY **GORDON WRIGHT** STYLING BY **ANGELA RIDGE** PHOTOGRAPH BY **GRAEME WYLLIE**

Serves 6 – 8 **EASY** 5 hrs 30 mins

THE FLAVOUR COMBINATIONS

475g mixed dried fruit
125ml (½ cup) rooibos/honeybush tea
100g brown sugar
65g butter + extra, to grease
2,5ml (½ tsp) bicarbonate of soda
1 egg, lightly beaten
30ml (2 tbsp) brandy + extra, to douse
60g cake flour
70g self-raising flour
5ml (1 tsp) ground cinnamon
2,5ml (½ tsp) nutmeg
2,5ml (½ tsp) ground cloves
60ml (¼ cup) walnuts, roughly chopped
5 silver coins, washed thoroughly

custard, to serve

HOW TO DO IT

1 Place the fruit in a large saucepan with the tea, sugar and butter. Stir constantly over high heat until the butter has melted and the sugar has dissolved. Bring to a boil, reduce the heat and simmer, uncovered, for 5 minutes.

2 Stir in the bicarbonate of soda, remove from heat and set aside to cool.

3 Add the beaten egg and brandy to the fruit mixture, and stir to combine.

4 Sift together the flours and spices, and add the walnuts. Add the sifted flour mixture to the fruit mixture and stir until combined. Drop in the coins and stir further.

5 Grease a large pudding basin with a little butter and spoon the mixture in. Cover with a tight-fitting lid or greased aluminium foil and tie securely with string. Place the pudding in a large saucepan with enough water to come halfway up the side of the bowl or pudding cloth. Cover and boil gently for 5 hours, replenishing the water occasionally as it evaporates.

6 After the pudding has been steamed, keep it in a cool, dry place for several weeks or longer. This improves it immensely.

7 On Christmas Day, steam the pudding for a few more hours. Turn it out onto a serving plate, douse in brandy and set alight. Once the flames subside, serve with custard. Those who find the lucky coins get to make a wish!

*Add a little extra brandy to the recipe and flambé
it just before serving. Very dramatic!*

Raspberry and shortbread ice-cream log with toasted marshmallow

RECIPE, STYLING AND PHOTOGRAPH BY **KATELYN WILLIAMS**

Serves 12 **EASY** 45 mins +
4 hrs, to freeze

THE FLAVOUR COMBINATIONS
3 large eggs, separated
60ml (¼ cup) castor sugar
300g mascarpone, softened
5ml (1 tsp) vanilla extract
200g raspberries + extra, frozen,
to garnish
200g butter-shortbread
finger biscuits

TOPPING
4 egg whites, at room temperature
120g castor sugar

HOW TO DO IT

1 Line a standard loaf tin with greased cling film. Beat the 3 egg yolks and 60ml (¼ cup) castor sugar with an electric beater until pale. Add the mascarpone and vanilla and beat until smooth.

2 In a separate bowl, whisk the 3 egg whites to soft peaks, then gently fold into the mascarpone mixture. Spoon into the loaf tin, scattering the raspberries into the mixture as you go. Top with the shortbread fingers, cover and freeze until firm, about 4 hours.

3 For the marshmallow topping, whisk the 4 egg whites in a bowl set over a pot of simmering water until they reach soft-peak stage. Add the 120g castor sugar gradually and beat until completely dissolved and the marshmallow is hot to the touch. Remove from heat and beat until cool.

4 When ready to serve, dip the mould with the ice-cream log once into boiling water, then turn out onto a plate. (Keep frozen until ready to serve.) Spread or pipe the marshmallow topping over the ice cream and, just before serving, brown the meringue using a blowtorch. Garnish with extra frozen raspberries.

FRUIT & VEGETABLE
SEASONALITY CHART

January

apricots	litchis
artichokes	mange tout
asparagus	mangoes
aubergines	mulberries
baby corn	mushrooms
baby marrow	nectarines
bananas	pattypans
beans	papayas
beetroot	peaches
blueberries	pineapples
cherries	pomegranates
figs	spinach
granadillas	strawberries
grapes	tomatoes
guavas	watermelons

February

apples	mealies
artichokes	melons
asparagus	peaches
baby marrows	pears
beans	peppers
beetroot	plums
berries	pomegranates
blueberries	radishes
chives	red onions
figs	rhubarb
granadillas	spinach
grapes	strawberries
mangoes	tomatoes

March

apples	mange tout
aubergines	mangoes
avocados	papayas
baby marrows	peaches
beans	pears
beetroot	peppers
blueberries	plums
cabbage	pomegranates
celery	spinach
figs	strawberries
granadillas	tomatoes
grapes	watermelons

April

apples	figs
avocados	gooseberries
baby marrows	granadillas
beans	leeks
beetroot	pears
broccoli	peppers
cabbage	pomegranates
cauliflower	spinach
celery	tomatoes

May

apples	gooseberries
avocados	Hubbard squash
baby marrows	leeks
beans	mandarins
beetroot	mushrooms
broccoli	papayas
Brussels sprouts	parsnips
butterbeans	pears
cabbage	persimmons
cauliflower	radishes
celery	spinach
figs	sweet peppers

June

apples	leeks
avocados	limes
beetroot	mandarins
broccoli	mushrooms
cabbage	naartjies
cauliflower	oranges
celery	parsnips
dates	papayas
gooseberries	pears
granadillas	persimmons
grapefruits	spinach

July

cabbage	kiwifruits
cauliflower	leeks
celeriac	mandarins
celery	mushrooms
gooseberries	papayas
granadillas	parsnips
grapefruits	persimmons
kale	sweet peppers

August

asparagus	granadillas
avocados	grapefruits
baby marrows	guavas
beans	kiwifruits
beetroot	leeks
broccoli	mandarins
cabbage	mushrooms
cauliflower	nectarines
celery	papayas
figs	parsnips
gooseberries	persimmons

September

apples	dates
asparagus	gooseberries
avocados	grapefruits
baby marrows	kiwifruits
bananas	leeks
beetroot	mushrooms
berries	papayas
cabbage	parsnips
cauliflower	strawberries
celery	tomatoes

October

artichokes	leeks
asparagus	mange tout
avocados	marrows
beans	mealies
beetroot	mushrooms
blueberries	parsnips
broccoli	peppers
cauliflower	rhubarb
celery	spinach
cherries	strawberries
gooseberries	tomatoes
grapefruits	turnips
kiwifruits	watercress

November

apricots	mange tout
artichokes	mealies
asparagus	mushrooms
aubergines	parsnips
avocados	papayas
baby marrows	peaches
beetroot	plums
blueberries	spinach
Brussels sprouts	strawberries
cherries	sweet peppers
grapes	tomatoes
leeks	watermelons

December

apricots	mangoes
artichokes	mushrooms
asparagus	nectarines
bananas	papayas
beans	peaches
blueberries	peppers
cherries	plums
figs	raspberries
grapes	spinach
guavas	strawberries
litchis	tomatoes
mange tout	watercress

QUANTITY CONVERSION CHART

We've selected the ingredients we thought most useful to be converted for everyday and special-occasion cooking and baking, and have put together a comprehensive volume-to-weight conversion chart for your convenience. We've carefully weighed out each ingredient in our test kitchen and we hope our conversion chart will be very useful in your home kitchen. Because all ingredients have differing densities, 1 cup of one ingredient will not be equal in weight for the same volume of another ingredient – hence the importance of a conversion chart. Our chart will also be handy when it comes to those recipes on the pages where the originator has not provided conversions.

GELATINE

To convert gelatine leaves to powdered gelatine, or vice versa, just use the same weight of gelatine. Simply, this means a standard 2g leaf of gelatine can be replaced by 2g powdered gelatine. If your leaf is equal to 3g, use 3g powdered gelatine. It is important to remember, however, that leaf gelatine sets your liquid clear, whereas powdered gelatine results in a murky appearance.

INGREDIENT	QUANTITY (VOLUME)	QUANTITY (WEIGHT)
BAKING		
Baking powder	5ml (1 tsp)	5g
Bicarbonate of soda	5ml (1 tsp)	7g
Cocoa powder	15ml (1 tbsp)	7g
Coconut, desiccated	250ml (1 cup)	95g
Coffee granules	15ml (1 tbsp)	5g
Cream of tartar	5ml (1 tsp)	5g
Custard powder	15ml (1 tbsp)	10g
Gelatine, powdered	5ml (1 tsp)	4g
Milk, powdered	250ml (1 cup)	115g
Yeast, dried	5ml (1 tsp)	4g
Yeast, fresh	5ml (1 tsp)	5g
BREADCRUMBS		
Breadcrumbs, brown, dried	250ml (1 cup)	55g
Breadcrumbs, brown, fresh	250ml (1 cup)	80g
Breadcrumbs, white, dried	250ml (1 cup)	55g
Breadcrumbs, white, fresh	250ml (1 cup)	65g
Breadcrumbs, panko	250ml (1 cup)	85g
Breadcrumbs, shop-bought	250ml (1 cup)	110g
CHEESES		
Bocconcini mozzarella, torn	250ml (1 cup)	200g
Cheddar, grated	250ml (1 cup)	125g
Cottage cheese, chunky	250ml (1 cup)	245g
Cottage cheese, creamed	250ml (1 cup)	225g
Cream cheese	250ml (1 cup)	235g
Feta cheese, crumbled	250ml (1 cup)	145g
Goat's cheese, crumbled	250ml (1 cup)	145g
Mascarpone	250ml (1 cup)	150g
Mozzarella, grated	250ml (1 cup)	127g
Parmesan, grated	250ml (1 cup)	100g
Ricotta, crumbled	250ml (1 cup)	170g

DAIRY

Butter	250ml (1 cup)	225g
Buttermilk	250ml (1 cup)	255g
Cream, fresh	250ml (1 cup)	255g
Crème fraîche	250ml (1 cup)	235g
Custard, shop-bought	250ml (1 cup)	270g
Double-thick cream	250ml (1 cup)	245g
Ice cream	250ml (1 cup)	195g
Milk	250ml (1 cup)	250g
Sour cream	250ml (1 cup)	235g
Yoghurt	250ml (1 cup)	250g

DRIED AND PRESERVED FRUIT AND VEGETABLES

Apple cubes, dried	250ml (1 cup)	85g
Apple rings, dried	250ml (1 cup)	85g
Cake mix	250ml (1 cup)	160g
Cherries, glacé, drained	250ml (1 cup)	200g
Citrus peel, candied	250ml (1 cup)	150g
Coconut flakes, dried	250ml (1 cup)	60g
Cranberries, dried	250ml (1 cup)	130g
Dates, dried	250ml (1 cup)	155g
Figs, dried	250ml (1 cup)	150g
Ginger, candied, drained	15ml (1 tbsp)	20g
Glacé fruit, mixed, chopped	250ml (1 cup)	170g
Goji berries, dried	250ml (1 cup)	110g
Mango strips, dried	250ml (1 cup)	95g
Mixed dried fruit, chopped	250ml (1 cup)	170g
Mushrooms, dried	250ml (1 cup)	35g
Peach halves, dried	250ml (1 cup)	125g
Pear halves, dried	250ml (1 cup)	175g
Pomegranate rubies, dried	250ml (1 cup)	165g
Pineapple, dried	250ml (1 cup)	140g
Prunes, dried	250ml (1 cup)	200g
Raisins	250ml (1 cup)	170g
Sultanas	250ml (1 cup)	160g

EGGS

Eggs, whole, beaten	250ml (1 cup)	255g
Egg yolks	250ml (1 cup)	260g
1 Egg yolk, large		18g
1 Egg yolk, extra-large		18g
1 Egg yolk, jumbo		18g
1 Egg white, large		36g
Egg whites	250ml (1 cup)	245g
1 Egg white, extra-large		38g
1 Egg white, jumbo		40g
1 Egg, whole, large, no shell		54g
1 Egg, whole, extra-large, no shell		56g
1 Egg, whole, jumbo, no shell		58g

FATS

Avocado oil	250ml (1 cup)	205g
Canola oil	250ml (1 cup)	210g
Coconut oil	250ml (1 cup)	220g
Duck fat	250ml (1 cup)	215g
Lard	250ml (1 cup)	220g
Margarine	250ml (1 cup)	235g
Olive oil	250ml (1 cup)	220g
Suet, dried, shredded	250ml (1 cup)	130g
Sunflower oil	250ml (1 cup)	215g

FLOURS

Almond, ground	250ml (1 cup)	120g
Bread flour	250ml (1 cup)	150g
Cake flour	250ml (1 cup)	150g
Chickpea flour	250ml (1 cup)	150g
Coconut flour	250ml (1 cup)	110g
Cornflour	15ml (1 tbsp)	10g
Mealie-meal, uncooked	250ml (1 cup)	195g
Self-raising flour	250ml (1 cup)	150g
Semolina	250ml (1 cup)	180g
Wholewheat flour	250ml (1 cup)	155g

FRUITS

Apple, chopped	250ml (1 cup)	130g
Apple, grated	250ml (1 cup)	195g
Banana, mashed	250ml (1 cup)	245g
Berries, mixed, frozen	250ml (1 cup)	155g
Blueberries, fresh	250ml (1 cup)	130g
Gooseberries, fresh	250ml (1 cup)	175g
Pineapple, chopped	250ml (1 cup)	150g
Raspberries, fresh	250ml (1 cup)	150g
Strawberries, fresh, whole	250ml (1 cup)	145g

GRAINS, BEANS, LEGUMES AND RICE

Arborio rice, uncooked	250ml (1 cup)	210g
Barley, pearl	250ml (1 cup)	200g
Basmati rice, uncooked	250ml (1 cup)	210g
Bulgar wheat	250ml (1 cup)	190g
Beans, red speckled, dried	250ml (1 cup)	170g
Beans, white, dried	250ml (1 cup)	170g
Chickpeas, dried	250ml (1 cup)	200g
Jasmine rice, uncooked	250ml (1 cup)	190g
Lentils, dried	250ml (1 cup)	210g
Oats, rolled	250ml (1 cup)	120g
Peas, split, dried	250ml (1 cup)	215g
Quinoa, uncooked	250ml (1 cup)	200g
Sago	250ml (1 cup)	185g
Samp, uncooked	250ml (1 cup)	200g
Sushi rice, uncooked	250ml (1 cup)	225g

LIQUIDS

Black coffee	250ml (1 cup)	250g
Coconut cream	250ml (1 cup)	260g
Coconut milk	250ml (1 cup)	255g
Fruit juice	250ml (1 cup)	250g
Nut milk	250ml (1 cup)	230g
Water	250ml (1 cup)	250g

NON-PERISHABLES

Anchovy fillets, drained	15ml (1 tbsp)	25g
Baked beans, tinned	250ml (1 cup)	280g
Condensed milk	250ml (1 cup)	315g
Corn, creamed, tinned	250ml (1 cup)	240g
Corn, tinned, drained	250ml (1 cup)	175g
Olives, drained	250ml (1 cup)	170g
Olives, drained and pitted	250ml (1 cup)	110g
Pineapple, tinned, crushed	250ml (1 cup)	280g
Sun-dried tomatoes, marinated and drained	250ml (1 cup)	180g
Tomato paste	15ml (1 tbsp)	20g
Tomatoes, chopped, tinned	250ml (1 cup)	240g
Tomatoes, whole baby, tinned	250ml (1 cup)	250g
Tomatoes, whole, tinned	250ml (1 cup)	235g
Tuna, drained	250ml (1 cup)	100g

NUTS AND SEEDS

Almonds, raw	250ml (1 cup)	155g
Brazil nuts, raw	250ml (1 cup)	155g
Cashew nuts, raw	250ml (1 cup)	145g
Chia seeds, raw	250ml (1 cup)	170g
Flaxseeds, raw	250ml (1 cup)	155g
Hazelnuts, raw	250ml (1 cup)	145g
Macadamia nuts, raw	250ml (1 cup)	150g
Mixed nuts, raw	250ml (1 cup)	140g
Peanuts and raisins	250ml (1 cup)	155g
Peanuts, roasted	250ml (1 cup)	150g
Pecan nuts, raw	250ml (1 cup)	100g
Pine nuts, raw	250ml (1 cup)	145g
Pistachios, raw and shelled	250ml (1 cup)	130g
Pistachios, raw and unshelled	250ml (1 cup)	110g
Poppy seeds, raw	250ml (1 cup)	145g
Psyllium seed husk, raw	250ml (1 cup)	150g
Pumpkin seeds, raw	250ml (1 cup)	140g
Sesame seeds, raw	250ml (1 cup)	160g
Sunflower seeds, raw	250ml (1 cup)	140g
Walnuts, raw	250ml (1 cup)	95g

PASTA AND NOODLES

Couscous, uncooked	250ml (1 cup)	190g
Elbow macaroni, uncooked	250ml (1 cup)	130g
Farfalle (bow ties), uncooked	250ml (1 cup)	60g
Macaroni, uncooked	250ml (1 cup)	110g
Orzo, uncooked	250ml (1 cup)	190g
Penne, uncooked	250ml (1 cup)	95g
Corkskrew pasta, uncooked	250ml (1 cup)	80g
Shells, medium	250ml (1 cup)	90g
Spaghetti, fresh, uncooked	250ml (1 cup)	70g
Tagliatelle, fresh, uncooked	250ml (1 cup)	80g
Udon noodles, fresh, uncooked	250ml (1 cup)	135g
Vermicelli, uncooked	250ml (1 cup)	40g

SAUCES AND CONDIMENTS

Chutney	250ml (1 cup)	280g
HP sauce	250ml (1 cup)	130g
Mayonnaise	250ml (1 cup)	225g
Olive tapenade	125ml (½ cup)	125g
Pesto	15ml (1 tbsp)	20g
Soya sauce	250ml (1 cup)	135g
Sweet-chilli sauce	250ml (1 cup)	140g
Tomato sauce	250ml (1 cup)	130g
Worcestershire sauce	250ml (1 cup)	245g

SUGARS

Brown sugar	250ml (1 cup)	220g
Caramel sugar	250ml (1 cup)	205g
Castor sugar	250ml (1 cup)	225g
Coconut blossom sugar	250ml (1 cup)	160g
Demerara sugar	250ml (1 cup)	150g
Icing sugar	250ml (1 cup)	145g
Muscovado sugar	250ml (1 cup)	190g
Treacle sugar	250ml (1 cup)	230g
White sugar	250ml (1 cup)	220g

Apricot jam	15ml (1 tbsp)	25g
Golden syrup	15ml (1 tbsp)	25g
Honey	15ml (1 tbsp)	25g
Glucose, liquid	15ml (1 tbsp)	375g
Maple syrup	15ml (1 tbsp)	30g
Molasses	15ml (1 tbsp)	30g
Strawberry jam	15ml (1 tbsp)	25g

VEGGIES

Aubergine, raw, chopped	250ml (1 cup)	115g
Beetroot, peeled, raw, chopped	250ml (1 cup)	150g
Butternut, raw, peeled and chopped	250ml (1 cup)	130g
Carrots, peeled, raw, chopped	250ml (1 cup)	150g
Carrots, peeled, grated	250ml (1 cup)	115g
Celery, chopped	250ml (1 cup)	110g
Cucumber, chopped	250ml (1 cup)	150g
Cucumber, grated	250ml (1 cup)	185g
Garlic, peeled and minced	15ml (1 tbsp)	10g
Ginger, peeled and minced	15ml (1 tbsp)	15g
Onion, peeled and chopped	250ml (1 cup)	135g
Peas, frozen, thawed	250ml (1 cup)	130g
Rhubarb, fresh, chopped	250ml (1 cup)	120g
Tomatoes, fresh, chopped	250ml (1 cup)	180g
Tomatoes, fresh, seeded and diced	250ml (1 cup)	210g

Recipe index